Your Towns and Cities in

City of London
in the Great War

'A company man to my right was too slow in getting on his helmet; he sank to the ground, clutching at his throat, and after a few sporadic twisting's, West died. It was horrible to see him die, but we were powerless to help him. In the corner of a traverse, a little muddy dog, one of the company's pets, was lying dead with his two paws over his nose.'

'Gas attack, 1916,' Eye Witness to History, www.eyewitnesstohistory.com (1999)

* * *

About the Author

Stephen is a happily retired police officer having served with Essex Police as a constable for thirty years between 1983 and 2013. He is married to Tanya. His two sons, Luke and Ross, were members of the armed forces, collectively having served five tours of Afghanistan between 2008 and 2013. Both of them were injured on their first tours which led to the publication of his first book; *Two Sons in a Warzone – Afghanistan: The True Story of a Father's Conflict*, which was published in October 2010. His teenage daughter, Aimee, is still at school. Both of his grandfathers survived the First World War, one with the Royal Irish Rifles, the other in the Mercantile Navy.

Stephen co-wrote a book published in August 2012, entitled *German POW Camp 266 – Langdon Hills* and has co-written three crime thrillers which were published between 2010 and 2012. He has also written other books for Pen & Sword Books, many of which are part of the Towns and Cities collection, which commemorate the sacrifices made by young men during the First World War.

Your Towns and Cities in the Great War

City of London
in the Great War

Stephen Wynn

Pen & Sword
MILITARY

First published in Great Britain in 2016 by
PEN & SWORD MILITARY
an imprint of
Pen and Sword Books Ltd
47 Church Street
Barnsley
South Yorkshire S70 2AS

ISBN 978 1 47382 859 9

A CIP record for this book is available from the British Library

Printed and bound in England
by CPI Group (UK) Ltd, Croydon, CR0 4YY

Typeset in Times New Roman by Chic Graphics

Pen & Sword Books Ltd incorporates the imprints of
Pen & Sword Archaeology, Atlas, Aviation, Battleground, Discovery,
Family History, History, Maritime, Military, Naval, Politics, Railways,
Select, Social History, Transport, True Crime, Claymore Press,
Frontline Books, Leo Cooper, Praetorian Press, Remember When,
Seaforth Publishing and Wharncliffe.

For a complete list of Pen and Sword titles please contact
Pen and Sword Books Limited
47 Church Street, Barnsley, South Yorkshire, S70 2AS, England
E-mail: enquiries@pen-and-sword.co.uk
Website: www.pen-and-sword.co.uk

Contents

Acknowledgements

I would like to say thank you to the following individuals for the help and assistance they provided in the completion of this book.

Many thanks to Roni Wilkinson for sourcing and providing me with a selection of the photographs that appear in this book, along with his advice, words of wisdom and calming influence.

I would like to thank Kate Jarman, the Deputy Archivist at St Batholomew's Hospital Archives and Museum, for her time, assistance, and for allowing me to view the hospital's staffing records (1914–1918). Part of the typescript of Emma Wilson's autobiography, *Those Were the Days*, which described her time as a probationer nurse at St Bartholomew's Hospital during the First World War, along with other historical documentation covering the same period.

Last but by no means least, I would like to thank my wife, Tanya, for her continued support and assistance, not only in my writing, but in the time she spent sourcing documentation and post cards for use in this book, as well as quite a few cups of tea that she provided along the way.

Prologue

The City of London has a rich and interesting history waiting to be rediscovered round every corner and down every street. A lot of it remains almost anonymous to most people, unless they happen to like history in general. A statue or a monument to a great general from a previous era, a war memorial remembering the fallen from a more recent war or a building that had once been important are all there, passed everyday by thousands of people.

The number of men who either came from the City of London or who served in one of the capital's numerous regiments ran into tens of thousands, many of whom were sadly either killed or wounded. The Tower of London was a barracks, an ammunition store, a prison, a recruiting station, a military hospital and a location where German spies were shot for their war time activities on the British mainland.

Although there were well over three hundred hospitals in London which catered for wounded soldiers and officers, who had been sent back to the UK to have their wounds treated, there was only one, St Bartholomew's, that was actually situated in the City of London.

Recruitment centres sprang up all over London on the outbreak of war, to cater for the large numbers of men from the capital who wanted to enlist, with more than enough regiments only too happy and willing to accept them.

A brief history of the City of London

For most books writing such a chapter would be a relatively straight forward thing to do, mainly because very few towns and cities have histories dating back over 2,000 years, but London's history is long and rich and deserves a brief mention. As best we know the name of London dates from the time of Roman Britain in the first century, in around 50 AD when it was established as the settlement of Londinium, serving as a major trading centre for the Roman Empire, sitting as it does on the banks of the River Thames, although it wasn't the capital of the country then; it would be the twelfth century before it held that position.

By 100 AD London's population had grown in size to around 60,000 people, making it one of the most densely populated cities in the Roman Empire at that time. Emperor Hadrian visited in around 122 AD, and between 190 and 225 AD, the Romans built the London Wall, which was a defensive structure that covered the landward side of the city. The wall was a massive structure by any standards, stretching as it did for about three miles in length. It was twenty feet in height and some eight feet thick. It would survive intact for another 1,600 years and parts of it can still be seen today at the side of Tower Hill.

Over the years London would see many changes. The Romans eventually upped and left it to its own devices in 410. The ninth century saw frequent Viking invasions, especially from 830 onwards, with London being sacked in 842 and once again in 851. It wasn't until 886, when King Alfred the Great triumphed over the Danes, that London once again came back under English rule, which is where it stayed until 1013. Once again the Danes took control of the Country, whose power it remained under until 1042.

The Battle of Hastings in 1066 saw William the Conqueror, Duke of Normandy take control of the country when he was subsequently crowned in Westminster Abbey. It was during this time that the construction of the Tower of London began. The Tower was stormed in 1381 during the Peasant's Revolt, when a group of rebels led by Wat Tyler, had brought their fight to London, culminating in the execution of the Lord Chancellor, the Lord Treasurer and Archbishop Simon Sudbury.

The Black Death swept across Europe between 1346 and 1352, resulting in an estimated 75 to 200 million deaths. London's population at the time was estimated to be roughly 80,000, half of which were killed during the epidemic.

Henry Vlll's dissolution of the monasteries began in 1530 and had a profound effect on the City of London. In that year the estimated population of London was 50,000. By 1605 it had risen to 225,000 with people being attracted to the ever growing metropolis by its rising wealth.

During the English Civil War (1642–1651), London sided with the Parliamentarians who finally won the day with victory at the Battle of Worcester on 3 September 1651.

The Great Fire of London started on Sunday 2 September 1666. It would be Thursday 6 September before it was finally brought under control, by which time 60% of the City of London had been destroyed by the fire. Although the loss of property was huge, only sixteen people lost their lives. The Rebuilding of London Act 1666 allowed for future buildings in London to be built of stone or brick. The only wood allowed in their construction was for doors, window frames and shop fronts. St Paul's Cathedral was completely destroyed and the building standing now was completed in 1708 to designs by Christopher Wren.

The Bow Street Runners, London's first ever full time professional Police force, was established in 1750, working out of Bow Street Magistrates Court. The Metropolitan Police Force were formed in 1829, making them one of the first Police forces in the country, the brain child of the then Home Secretary and future Prime Minister, Sir Robert Peel.

Buckingham Palace, then named Buckingham House, was acquired by King George III in 1762 from the Duke of Buckingham.

By 1800 as London grew in stature, economic importance and wealth, so did its population, to over one million people. Life in the city wasn't good for most, because they were controlled by overcrowding, poverty, a lack of sanitation and an ever increasing crime rate.

The railway finally came to London in 1836, with a line from London Bridge to Greenwich. By 1863, work had begun on the London Underground.

By 1900 and the birth of the twentieth century, the population of London had risen to a staggering six and a half million people.

During the First World War, London experienced bombing raids by German Zeppelins, which killed some 700 people and injured hundreds more. When fifty tons of TNT at the Munitions factory in Silvertown exploded on Friday 19 January 1917, it killed seventy-three people and injured over 400.

CHAPTER 1

Outbreak of the War, Buckingham Palace, the Stock Exchange

The evening of Monday 3 August 1914 was pleasant enough, as crowds of people made their way into the centre of London as the nation drew closer to the impending outbreak of war.

The numbers of people were no doubt even larger than might be expected, due to it being a Bank Holiday. During the day, there had been an estimated 60,000 people in the city as the expectation of war moved ever closer to reality. As the evening approached, many started making their way home, but not all did. As the day passed and the evening took over, the crowds who had initially converged on the Houses of Parliament, an estimated 10,000, made the short journey from Parliament Square, along Bird Cage Walk, to the gates of Buckingham Palace, waving hats and handkerchiefs as they went. The feeling in the air was one of excitement and national fervour as the emotion of the moment took hold, leading to spontaneous outburst of cheering and the singing of the national anthem.

With the threat of war having been a strong possibility for some time, it would have been more of a shock to people if it hadn't begun. These were changing times, both nationally and internationally; the population could sense this and wanted to be part of it. Going into the city that evening was not just about soaking up the atmosphere and partying on into the night, people wanted to be there to show their support for the king and queen at what was a difficult time. The crowds of revellers were not to be disappointed, as the Royal couple responded by appearing on the main balcony at the front of Buckingham Palace along with the Prince of Wales and Princess Mary, to take in the cheers of the buoyant crowd.

Rich and poor, businessmen and workers all stood side by side in their support for the inevitable that was soon to become a reality. The feeling of national unity and togetherness cut across all levels of society and unified everybody in a common cause. Such were the heightened feelings of national pride on display that day, that when a well-meaning individual started handing out leaflets proffering 'peace at any price', he quickly had to be rescued by the Police who feared that he might be seriously injured by the crowds who undoubtedly had different ideas on the matter than he did.

One of the questions which hung in the air was 'are we prepared enough'. Although Germany was prepared regarding manpower, it did not appear that was the case when it came to food supplies, having not made any substantial stockpiles, which was quite surprising when she had been manoeuvring towards war for some time, suggesting that there was no belief on Germany's part that the war was either going to last that long or that Britain would so readily become embroiled in it.

At the outbreak of war, the Germany army comprised some 700,000 men, but within a week those figures had risen to 3.8 million when they called up their reservists, having had conscription for short term military service in place for some years. After having completed their period of conscription, German men were then placed on a reserve list for such an eventuality as the First World War.

Compare these figures with what Britain had at the same time. Her army at home consisted of 138,000 men who were on the active list, with a further 146,000 in the Reserves. There was also the Special Reserve, which consisted of 63,000 men, as well as the Territorial Force which provided another 250,000 men. On top of this, Britain had 78,000 men serving in India as well as a further 41,000 stationed in Egypt and numerous colonies around the world, not forgetting the 100,000 men serving in her Navy, and on top of this were the armies of the other Commonwealth countries.

Even though it was universally accepted that Germany had a strong and disciplined army, possibly the best that there was throughout all of Europe, Britain more than matched this when it came to the power of her sea-going fleet, which was unrivalled on the high seas of the world.

At 12.15 am on Wednesday 5 August 1914 the following announcement was issued at the Foreign Office in London, sixty-three words that would change the world for ever.

> 'Owing to the summary rejection by the German Government of the request made by His Majesty's Government for assurances that the neutrality of Belgium would be respected, His Majesty's Ambassador in Berlin has received his passports, and his Majesty's Government has declared to the German Government that a state of war exists between Great Britain and Germany as from 11pm on August 4.'

Large crowds had gathered in Whitehall and Trafalgar Square, a magnet for national fervour at such times, to greet the expected news with applause and enthusiastic approval. Although with the benefit of hindsight one hundred years on, this might seem a somewhat unusual reaction to such news, in the early years of the twentieth century, it was quite a normal response, and with the levels of tension and expectation having risen so considerably over the previous weeks and days, the announcement of war must have been received with a certain feeling of relief.

Wednesday 5 August 1914 saw adverts in the national daily newspapers encouraging young men to join the Army.

Your King and Country need you

'Will you answer your country's call? Each day is fraught with the gravest possibilities, and at this very moment the Empire is on the brink of the greatest war in the history of the world.

'In this crisis your country calls on all her young unmarried men to rally round the flag and enlist in the ranks of her Army.

'If you are unmarried and between 18 and 30 years old, will you answer your country's call and go to the nearest recruiter whose address you can get at any Post Office and Join the Army today?'

It wasn't just soldiers that the War Office were looking for, they were looking for all kinds of different tradesmen. In no particular order of importance they required: motor-cyclists, clerks, labourers, drivers, butchers, bakers, tailors, saddlers, painters, blacksmiths, coppersmiths, electricians, pattern makers, moulders, wheelers and turners, to name but a few. This really was an army on the move.

Surgeons and doctors were badly needed to enlist in the Royal Army Medical Corps. They had to be registered practitioners and prepared to provide their service for 12 months or until they were no longer required. Gentlemen who enlisted would be granted the temporary rank of lieutenant, but there was no official criteria laid down as to how it was possible to determine what allowed a man to class himself as a gentleman. Maybe it was simply his claim to being a gentleman that made him so, or the tone of his voice or the manner in which he spoke that determined the outcome.

The following article appeared in the *Evening Despatch* on Saturday 8 August 1914. It was a reminder, as if any was required, that life in the City of London had just changed.

LONDON POLICE ARMED

'All the officers in the City of London Police force above the rank of Sergeant are armed with the latest pattern quick firing revolvers and ball cartridges.

'Constables on special duty are being similarly armed. Each police station has been supplied with sufficient weapons to arm every constable in the force.'

In the same edition of the newspaper was a report of an incident involving a Territorial soldier from the City of London, who had a narrow escape from death, highlighting how dangerous life had suddenly become because of the war and not just for those who were serving in theatres of war overseas.

Territorial Sergeant's Narrow Escape

'A Sergeant of the City of London Territorials has had an extraordinary double escape from injury or death while visiting the sentries on the London and South Western Railway between Weybridge and Walton. The Sergeant missed his footing and fell over a concrete bank on to the rails. A sentry hearing the noise, challenged, and getting no reply from the Sergeant who was dazed, fired. Fortunately the sergeant was not hit and was subsequently removed to hospital suffering from injuries to his arm.'

The content of the later conversation between the two soldiers, which it is naturally assumed took place, must have been a very interesting one to say the least. Sadly, neither the newspaper nor history recorded what was said.

Even though Buckingham Palace isn't actually in the City of London, it was at the very centre of celebrations at both the outset of the war as well as its end. Throughout the war the Palace was like a magnet for tens of thousands of well-wishers, day trippers and soldiers home on leave or those preparing to return to the Front, all hoping that they might just get a brief glimpse of the king or other members of the Royal family. Even though they might not have been aware of it at the time, the Royal family and Buckingham Palace really did provide a morale boost to the entire nation in those troubled times.

The *Western Mail* of Friday 7 August 1914 reported the following:

Prince of Wales to join Grenadier Guards on Active Service – Anxious to prove his Patriotism.

'The Western Mail understands that the Prince of Wales will join the Grenadier Guards forthwith, and will go with them upon active service. It is known that his Royal Highness, who joined the Navy and qualified for the rank of Lieutenant, has been keenly anxious to prove his patriotism by serving the King and country in the present grave crisis of the country's history, just as his brother Prince Albert, is doing in the First Battle Squadron of the Royal Navy.

'It is understood the Prince will go with them where the exigencies of the situation call.

'The Prince of Wales has consented to become treasurer of the National Relief Fund, and on Thursday night he issued the following appeal from Buckingham Palace.

'All must realise that the present time of deep anxiety will be followed by one of considerable distress among the people of this country least able to bear it. We most earnestly pray that their sufferings may be neither long nor bitter, but we cannot wait until the need presses heavily upon us; the means of relief must be ready in our hands. To allay anxiety will go some way to stay distress.

A national fund has been founded, and I am proud to act as its treasurer. My first duty is to ask for a generous and ready support, and I know that I shall not ask in vain. At such a moment we all stand by one another, and it is to the heart of the British people that I confidently make the most earnest appeal.

Edward.'

The Prince of Wales' appeal was followed by further appeals from Queen Mary as well as the Queen Mother, Queen Alexandra. The queen was in support of the Prince of Wales fund and the Queen Mother in respect of the Soldiers' and Sailors' Families Association which she had previously championed during the South African War of 1899-1902. Those wishing to support any of the Royal appeals were asked to send either a postal order or a cheque, made out to Coutts and Co, the Royal Bank of choice.

In the *Daily Mirror* dated 23 October 1915 George V made an appeal to his people for more men to join the armed forces, such was the need to ensure that his armies remained effective on the battlefield.

'To My People

'At this grave moment in the struggle between my people and a highly organised enemy who has transgressed the Laws of Nations and changed the ordinance that binds civilized Europe together, I appeal to you.

'I rejoice in my Empire's effort, and I feel pride in the voluntary response from my subjects all over the world who have sacrificed home, fortune, and life itself, in order that another may inherit the free Empire which their ancestors and mine have built.

'I ask you to make good these sacrifices. The end is not in sight. More men and yet more are wanted to keep my armies in the field, and through them to secure Victory and enduring peace.

'In ancient days the darkest moment has ever produced in men of our race, the sternest resolve. I ask you, men of all classes, to come forward voluntarily and take your share in the fight.

'In freely responding to my appeal, you will be giving your support to our brothers, who, for long months, have nobly upheld Britain's past traditions, and the glory of her arms.

'George.'

An article in the *Daily Mirror* dated Friday 10 December 1915, reported the following.

The King and VCs
Officer and Private receive coveted honour
at Buckingham Palace
Rescued on a Shovel

'Two VCs received their decoration from the King at an investiture which his majesty held at Buckingham Palace yesterday.

'One of the heroes was Lieutenant B H Geary, of the East Surrey Regiment, who won his coveted award in the memorable battle of Hill 60: and the other, Private Alfred Potts, of the Berkshire Yeomanry, whose conspicuous bravery and devotion to a wounded comrade in the Gallipoli peninsula gained him his distinction.

'Lieutenant Geary's case is a remarkable one. With his platoon he held a crater against repeated attacks, each of which was repulsed owing to his splendid bravery. He was severely wounded, a bullet passing through one side of his head to the other. As a consequence the sight of one eye is completely destroyed and the other so injured that he can only see objects at a certain angle. However, the plucky officer hopes yet to be able to perform more useful work, and after the war he proposes to enter the church.

'The official record of Private Potts' heroism is as follows: Although himself severely wounded in the thigh in the attack on a Hill on August 21 1915, he remained out over forty-eight hours under the Turkish trenches with a private of his regiment who was severely wounded and unable to move, although he himself could have returned to safety.

'Finally he fixed a shovel to the equipment of his wounded comrade and using this as a sledge he dragged him back over 600 yards to our lines, though fired at by the Turks on the way. He reached our trenches at about 9.30pm on August 23.

When Private Potts left the Palace he was surrounded and warmly congratulated by men of his own regiment who were waiting for him outside.'

Events in the City of London were also of interest all around the country. The *Huddersfield Daily Examiner* dated Wednesday 5 August 1914, reported the following.

PROCLAMATIONS READ
Enthusiasm in City of London
'Enthusiastic scenes were witnessed in the City this morning, when in the presence of a dense crowd, five Royal proclamations relating to the war were read from the steps of the Royal Exchange.'

Unfortunately the article didn't explain what each of the proclamations was about

With war imminent and a belief that businesses and other banking establishments who had loaned large sums of money would now look to call those loans in, the Stock Exchange, with the support of Parliament, decided that it was best to close for business at the end of July 1914; it did not re-open until 4 January 1915.

The *Daily Record* dated 27 August 1914 carried the following article about the Stock Exchange.

FINANCIAL NOTES
DEALINGS IN THE 'STREET' MARKET
'The rainy weather disturbed the unofficial Stock Exchange "street" market. A very small number of cash transactions were arranged at about the same prices as those of the past few days. Consols being 69 and a half, Canadian Pacifics 158, Unions 115, Mexican Eagle Oils 1 and a half, Chartereds 11s 6d, and De Beers 12.

'It is still impossible to forecast the reopening of the Stock Exchange, but a Government scheme may be formulated whereby security holders will be able to obtain loans on securities on reasonable.'

When it did reopen, with the war by then five months old, the exchange operated under very tough restrictions and with a lot fewer members, with over 1,000 of them having quit.

At the outbreak of the war, men from the London Stock Exchange, formed the 10th (Service) Battalion of the Royal Fusiliers, which was one of the Battalions of what was known as the New Army. It was formed in the City of London in August 1914 but it did not come under the control of the War Office. As a lot of the men who had joined the Battalion were stockbrokers who worked in the City, their nickname, not surprisingly was the Stockbrokers. Their Honorary Colonel was Sir Thomas Vansittart Bowater, who was the Lord Mayor of the City of London between 1913-14.

The Battalion first landed in Boulogne on 30 July 1915. Some 1,600 men initially enlisted, 408 of whom never came home. This was one of the forty-seven battalions that were raised by the Royal Fusiliers during the First World War.

The 10th Service (Stockbrokers) Battalion, formed part of the 111th Brigade, which was in turn part of the British 37th Division, who would spend the rest of the war fighting on the Western Front, taking part in such battles as the Somme in 1916, Pilkem Ridge, Menin Road Ridge, Polygon Wood and Passchendaele, throughout 1917 and those at Havrincourt, Cambrai and Sambre in 1918.

At the signing of the Armistice on 11 November 1918 the 37th Division was at Le Quesnoy. They had fought throughout the war with resilience, tenacity and pride and in doing so had seen a total of 29,969 of their number either killed, wounded or missing in action. By 19 March 1919, the last of the men of the 37th Division had been demobilized, and for them the war was finally over, well at least in a physical sense.

There is a War Memorial at the Stock Exchange to commemorate those members who died or were killed during the First World War. It was unveiled on 27 October 1922 by the 1st Earl of Balfour. As plain Arthur Balfour, he had been the Conservative prime minister between 1902 and 1905 as well as the Foreign Secretary between 1916 and

1919. The aptly named hymn *The Supreme Sacrifice* was sung by those in attendance and Buglers from the Honourable Artillery Company played the Last Post Reveille.

The list of those brave young men who made the ultimate sacrifice, most of whom weren't professional soldiers and who probably would never have joined the Armed Forces if it hadn't been because of the war, is as follows:

Arthur Leonard Victor Abbott
Phillips Montague Edwin Abbott
Montague Nathan Abrahams
Albert Reginald Knight Aitkens
Gordon Reuben Alexander
Charles Harrington Ardley
George Bertram Ashworth
Ronald Grantham Austin
Greville John Massey Bagot-Chester
Francis Cedric Balcombe
Leslie Arthur Balance
Herbert William Barnett
Maurice William Barstow
Richard Louis Whittington Bartlett
Geoffrey Edward Bassett
William Henry Bayless
Geoffrey Martyn Bazin
Frederick Barberry Bennett
Ernest J Bird
Roland Powell Birtles
George Dullam Blackman
Edwin Oswald Blakeway
Frederick Courtnay Boully
Russell William Bradberry
Richard William Braithwaite
Hugh Frederic G Bromley
Thomas Skilton Brown
Oswald Lee Buckoke
Robert Moyle Burman (DSO, MC, MID)

Joseph Octavius Abbott
John Arthur
John H Adams
Walter George Albu
George Jenner Andrew
Dumbreck Arthur
Francis Herbert Atkin
F Baker
Cecil Douglas Baker
Percy Balfour (DSO)
Walter James Barnes
Victor Baron Barnett
Claude Bartholomew (MC)
G E Bartram
Reginald Alan Battison
Edward Vincent Bayley
Harold Clifford Beard
Mowbray Bessell
William Ryder Bird
S Bishop
William Gordon Blackwell
George Wilson Borman
Richard Harvey Boys
William Arthur Bradley
J Brander
Arthur Edwin Bronsdon
Edward James Brunsden
E C Burgess (DCM)
Philip Burwood

Alfred Stanley Butchart

Herbert Montague Soame Carpenter

Henry Gordon Carter

Sidney Herbert Carter

William James Carter

Lionel Trevor Case

Ernest Rowland Chappell

Harry Brodrick Chinnery

Charles Douglas Clark

Charles Benjamin Clarke

Stewart Algernon Clarke

Walter John Clayton

Samuel Pepys Cockerell

Sidney Franklin Collin

Frank C Collingwood

Arthur Alfred James Collins

Lionel Drummond Collins

Edward Ralph Cooke

Leslie Howard Coombs

Henry Cormac-Walshe

David Henry Harman Cornfoot

William Ronald Corrie

Reginald Leyster Courtice

Laurence Edward Courtney

Tom Crafter

John William Archibald Craig

Cecil Crosley (MID)

E J Cross

Stanley Cundall

Edward Hedley Cuthbertson

James Alfred Daniels

Claude J Davies

John Sewell Davies

Robert Ffindon Davies

Sidney Alfred Davies

Cyril Vincente Davis

Norman D Davis

Frederick Clifton Dawkins (MC)

Wilfred Leedham Dawson

Frederick Robert De Levante

Leon Victor St Patrick De Landre-Grogan (MC)

Alan Frederick James De Rutzen

Henry Glanville Dennison

Robert William Lee Dodds

Francis Dodgson

John Henley Dodgson

Andrew Patrick Donald

William Richard Donovan

Graham Dudley Driver

Cyril Harry Dupe

John Vivian William Eccles

Francis Douglas Edmands

Leslie Morier Evans

Francis Cuthbert Evennett

Henry C Farnes

W Fielding

Douglas Gordon Fisher-Brown

Peter Fitch

Gordon Amhurst Forsyth

Ernest Franklyn (MSM)

Henry Oscar Franklyn

Alexander Evan Fraser

The Hon. Simon Fraser

George Cyril Freeman

Cecil Berkeley French

William Sigismund Friedberger

Philip Emlyn Friend

Gustave Albert Frymann

Frederic Furze

L A C Gale
John Charles Gardom
William Henry Geliot
John H Gibson
Alastair Stuart Gilmour
Laurence Vivian Glover
Ralph Edward Godin
Christopher Gerard Goschen
Fenton Weiss Graham
Frederick Hodskinson Gray
Victor St Patrick de Lande Grogan
  (MC)
Stanley George Groome
William Webb Hale
Geoffrey Evans Hall
Walter Hallett
John Latham Hampton
Reginald William Fowler Harding
Ernest Edward Harris
Leonard G Hartin
Albert Leonard Harvey
William John Weatherall
Sydney Harold Wilfred Herbage
James Bryan Hichens
William Frederick John Higgs
Wilfred Gurney Hoare

Richard Arthur Hornby
George C Hoskins
Laurence Walter Howcroft
Lestocq Hughes
Lawrence George Hummerstone
John Richards Hurlstone
Thomas Anderson Hyslop (MC)
Leslie Yardley Inman
Thomas Robinson Irving
Gerald Radcliffe Jackman
Ernest Edward James

William C Gantsman
George Charles Garland
Walter Leslie Gibbs
Geoffrey Giles
George Gibson
W E Godfrey
Harold Eastly Gordon
Alexander Cecil Graham
Ernest Charles Gransee
Victor William Gregory
Percy Grover

Leonard Alloway Groves
Bernard William Hall
Norman de Haviland Hall
Bertram E Hambro
Arthur William Harding
Evelyn Harper
J Harris
Frederick Lynn Hartley
Ronald Young Hedderwick
Franklyn Thomas Hemsley
Robert Bingley Herbert
Arthur Kendrick Hickman
Harold Salton Hilder
Walter John Gerald Hoare,
  (DSO)
Robert Henry Hose
Aubrey Finch How
J H Hubbard
Stanley Beavan Hughes
Edward Huntley
James Hyslop, (MC, MM)
Arthur Herbert Ingram
Ambrose Constantine Ionides

Charles George Jackson
Richard Arthur Brodie James

Reginald Robert Jenkinson

Thomas Henry Fielder Johnson (DSO)
David Harry Johnston
Ralph Bradbury Kay
Noel Keith
Lionel Victor Kent
Chester Winterbon Killby
George Montague King
John Stephen Raymond Lake
Sidney John Lane
Basil Herbert Last
Arthur C Lazarus
William Reginald Leathley
Raymond Litten

Sidney Henry Lowry (MC)
William David MacBeth
James Herbert Nengoe MacLeod
Henry Fairholm Manners
Charles Silverlock Marchant
Cyril B Martin
Leonard Burnett Martin
Walter Percival Martin
Peter Langton May
Archibald David McAfee
George McBean
James Hillman Miller
Walter Victor Mitchell
Maurice Moore
Harold Bolingbroke Mudie
Percy Simmons Murray
Arthur Plater Nasmith (DSO)
Robert Percy Nathan (MC)
Cuthbert St John Nevill
Nathaniel Halford Newman
Stuart Bertram Noakes
Herbert Joseph Oakenfell

Charles Mitchell Warren
  Jephson
J E Jones
Stanley Jopling
Claude Jeffery Keeping
B R Kelly
Frederick Roxburghe Ker
Cecil Molyneux Killik
Ernest Harold Kitchin
Wilfred Lawrence (MID)
Pelham Lang Grieve
Adolph Keith Lavarack
Charles Ralph Le Blanc-Smith
Horace Gordon Legg
Norman McGregor Lowe
  (DCM)
William Bullen Lund
Gilchrist Stanley MacLagan
Frank Laing Macrae
George Hewlett Mapp
William Marsh
Henry Lloyd Martin
Lionel Norman John Martin
H Matthews
Cecil Clarence Mays
Richard James McAllister
Ronald Meldrum
C H Mitchell
Malcolm Mitchison
Alfred James Morison
J B Munford
Walter Cecil Myatt
David Nathan
Leslie Alfred Needham
John Henry Gaythorne Nevill
Edgar Charles Newton
Guy Valentine Nossiter
Cyril Francis Harrison Oliver

Timothy Thomas O'Reardon
Joseph Henry Pack
Harold Anderson Pailthorpe (MID)
George Papier
Charles Frederick Pavitt (MC)
Laumann Saxe William Pearson
Herbert Richard Pelly
Charles Maurice Sewell Peters
Laurence Piper
George Eveleigh Plater
Edward Henry Pott
Leonard Frith Powell
Charles Ernest Proughten
Thomas Tannatt Pryce (VC, MC
  & Bar)
Harry Victor Ramsey
Douglas Rawlings
Stanley William Reacher
William Francis Reay
H D Reid
Frederick Henry Reynell
Nathan Bright Risley (MC)
Patrick Maitland Robertson-Ross

Leonard William Roddis
Cyril G Ross
James Ross
Eric Fay Salter
Harold Colenso Sarfas
Arthur Ferdinand Schneider
Charles Comyn Scott Scott-Gatty
Walter Vernon Shairp
Max Joseph Shaw
Archibald Edward Sheldon

Edward Hill Sheridan

John Wynton Shilcock

Lucien Eugene Oudin (MC)
Vernon Page (MC)
Lawrence Grant Palmer
Thomas Parker
Malcom Gerald Pawle
Sydney Edgar Peddle
Eric Frank Penn
Percy Vivian Philcox
Percy Douglas Pitt
Guy Bernard Poland
Harold Potter
E S Price
Frank Blashfield Ramsey
Maxwell Rabone

Rupert George Raw (DSO)
George Biddulp Rayner
Arthur James Read
Egbert Reid
Oscar Harold Reid
Roland Richards
Henry Fergus Robertson
Arthur Murdoch Maxwell
  Robertson-Walker (MID)
William Charles Herbert Rose
George William Ross
James Tarrell Russell
Geoffrey Evan Sanderson
Harold Oscar Saunders
Reginald Oscar Schwarz (MC)
Edward Seager
Montague de Mancha Shattock
Raymond Pugh Shaw
Samuel Gurney Sheppard
  (DSO)
William Frederick Temple
  Sheridan
George Albert Simmonds

Guy Bloxham Simmonds
Walter Septimus Simpson
Gordon Keith Smith (MC)
W A Smith
Kyrle Nalder Stephens

Edgcumbe Leopald Stiles
George Nicholas Strang
John Morton Tabor
Theodore Arthur Tapp (MC & Bar)
William Alfred Taylor
George R Thorpe
Frederick Trew
Arthur Thomas Turne
George Beaumont Tyser
Alan Francis Vertue
Edward Maxwell Vowler
Henry Norman Wal
William Thomas Ward
Cecil Alberic Hardy Warre
Reginald Watson
Henry Webber (MID)
Harold West
Edward Whinney
James Hugh Edendale Whitehead
Gordon Frederick Noble Wilkinson
David James E Willats
Ernest Willis
James Edward Holmes Wilson
Frank Thomas Winterbourn
Hector Frederick Wood (MC)
Austin Hale Woodbridge (MC)
Stanley George Woodbridge (MC
Samuel Herbert Woodward
Oswald Eric Wreford-Brown

Ernest Herbert Simpson
Albert Leonard Smith
Julian Martin Smith
Ronald B Stanley
Samuel Charles Stephens
   (MIDx2)
Charles Herbert Stock
Hubert Lionel Syer (MC)
William Clifford Taffs
Robert Sommers Tate
Geoffrey Owen Thomas
Albin George Tomkins
Harold Willis Troughton
Harold Robert Tyler
William Samuel Underhill
Algernon Hyde Villiers
George Wainmain (MM)
Henry H Wallace
George Phillip Ware
Charles Watson (MM)
John William Wattam
Harry George Welham (MC)
Herbert St John Carr West
George Whitaker
Nigel B Whitfield
N Wilkinson
Harry Ashley Willats
Arthur Leslie Wilson
George Henry Wilson (MC)
Charles Perceval Wood
John Patrick Hamilton Wood
Francis Joseph Woods
R D Wright
Reginald George Worley
Frank Thomas Writer (MM)

Reading through that list brings home the enormity of the true cost of war, because they are not just a list of faceless individuals, they were husbands, sons, fathers, uncles and brothers. Their loss was heartfelt by their family and friends at the time and their memories live on in the hearts and minds of their relatives who followed afterwards.

The majority of the men named on the list were officers, possibly the biggest concentration of military officers to come out of one organisation in the entire First World War. They served in numerous different regiments and corps from all over England, Scotland and Wales. Collectively, the men from the Stock Exchange who served during the war were awarded a total of forty-eight awards for gallantry, including one Victoria Cross, seven Distinguished Service Orders, two Distinguished Conduct Medals, one Military Service Medal, twenty-six Military Crosses, four Military Medals as well as eight men who were Mentioned in Despatches.

All of them rightly deserve to be mentioned for their actions of gallantry and bravery, but four in particular stand out.

Thomas Tannatt Pryce was a captain in the 4th Battalion, Grenadier Guards when he was killed in action on 13 April 1918 at Vieux Berquin, France, at the Battle of Hazebrouck. The *London Gazette* dated 21 May 1918 gave the following account of his actions that earned him the award of the Victoria Cross.

'For most conspicuous bravery, devotion to duty, and self-sacrifice when in command of a flank on the left of the Grenadier Guards. Having been ordered to attack a village he personally led forward two platoons working from house to house, killing some thirty of the enemy, seven of whom he killed himself. The next day he was occupying a position with some thirty to forty men, the remainder of his company having become casualties.

'As early as 8.15am his left flank was surrounded and the enemy was enfilading him. He was attacked no less than four times during the day, and each time beat off the hostile attack, killing many of the enemy. Meanwhile the enemy brought three field guns to within 300 yards of his line, and were firing over open sights and knocking his trench in. At 6.15 p.m., the enemy had worked to within sixty yards of his trench. He then called on his men, telling them to cheer and charge the enemy and fight to the last. Led by Captain Pryce, they left their trench and drove back the enemy with the bayonet some 100 yards. Half an hour later the enemy had again approached in stronger force. By this time Captain Pryce had only 17 men left, and every round of his ammunition had been fired. Determined that there should be no surrender, he once again led his men forward in a bayonet charge, and was last seen engaged in a fierce hand-to-hand struggle with overwhelming numbers of the enemy. With some forty men he had held back at least one enemy battalion for over ten hours. His company undoubtedly stopped the advance through the British line, and thus had great influence on the battle.'

Before enlisting in the army and becoming a lieutenant, with the 7th Battalion, South Lancaster Regiment, Henry Webber had worked for forty years on London's Stock Exchange. When the First World War began Henry Webber was already sixty-five years of age, the age when most men were thinking of retiring and putting their feet up, but not Henry; all he wanted to do was to enlist and do his bit. When Henry Webber was killed in action on 21 June 1916 he was sixty-seven years of age which made him the oldest known battle casualty of the First World War. During his war time service he was Mentioned in Despatches. He is buried in the Dartmoor Cemetery at Bercordel-Becourt which is situated in the Somme region of France.

Thomas Hyslop was a 2nd Lieutenant in the 10th Battalion attached to the 4th Battalion, Alexandra, Princess of Wales's Own (Yorkshire Regiment). His brother, James Hyslop, was a lieutenant with the 14th (County of London) Battalion (London Scottish), London Regiment. Both were awarded the Military Cross for their Bravery, with James also being awarded the Military Medal. Thomas, the younger of the two brothers at twenty-nine, was the first to die, killed in action on 22 March 1918. James was also killed in action on 5 November 1918, just six days before the signing of the Armistice. The brother's parents, John and Grace Hyslop, had the sad task of having to deal with the deaths of both of their sons in the space of only seven months.

CHAPTER 2

Recruitment, Lord Mayors 1914–1918

Recruitment in the early months and years of the First World War was almost on manic proportions as young men across the country rushed to enlist in the army so they could do their bit by serving king and country in their hour of need. Some of these men were looking for excitement, some for adventure, some were doing it out of honour and some just because they saw it as their basic duty.

The *Cambridge Evening Press* dated Friday 14 August 1914 reported the following in relation to recruitment.

Army recruitment poster by Alfred Leete.

'At a meeting of his Majesty's Lieutenants of the City of London at the Guildhall on Wednesday, a sum of £500 was voted towards the City of London Branch of the Red Cross Society. The meeting agreed to assist in every possible way with the enlistment of men for the Regular Army and Territorial Force.'

London was a particular hive of activity as far as recruitment went. By 31 August 1914, 34,730 men had joined up throughout London. By the end of the first week of September another 21,870 young men had followed in their footsteps and enlisted. As recruiting officers were paid for each man they enlisted, in some cases recruitment staff would turn a blind eye to those who might not quite be legally old enough to enlist.

Although not actually in the City of London, there were recruiting offices at Whitehall, Great Scotland Yard, Camberwell, Islington, Battersea, Fulham, and Marylebone. The 12th (Bermondsey) Battalion, East Surrey Regiment, had their main recruiting office at Rotherhithe Town Hall. The 10th Queens (Battersea) Service Battalion, had their recruiting depot at Lavender Hill Town Hall.

The Tower of London was where the 10th (Stockbrokers) Battalion of the Royal Fusiliers (City of London Regiment) were raised and sworn in, and by the end of August 1914, more than 1600 men had been recruited at the Tower, but sadly by the end of the war only 50 men out of the original group, were still on active service. Overall, the Battalion had suffered a total of 2,647 casualties. The original men who had enlisted in August 1914, were affectionately known as the 'Ditchers', because they had enlisted in the outside ditch or the moat at the Tower of London. The Stockbrokers Battalion, not only became one of the earliest Pals Battalions, but also became one of the 'poshest' and most affluent Battalions that there was.

The London Scottish Regiment whose headquarters was at 59, Buckingham Gate, Westminster, carried out their own recruitment from that address, which in 1912, had been used for the Titanic enquiry.

There were sixty-three headquarters and drill halls for London Territorial units in 1914, and it is highly likely that the initial recruitment for these regiments would have been held at those locations.

Peter Simkins' book, Kitchener's Army – The raising of the New Armies 1914-1916, records that all twenty-eight London Metropolitan town halls and their staff, were placed at the disposal of the War Office on 18 August 1914. The 23rd and 24th Battalions, Royal Fusiliers, had a recruiting office at the Hotel Cecil at 80, The Strand in London. There was a recruiting office for the New Armies at the Workingmen's College on Crowndale Road, Camden, and another at The Baths, Camberwell Green, London. The Royal West Kent Regiment had a recruiting centre at Frances Street, Woolwich, London.

As the war continued, so more and more men were required to go off and fight, which in turn meant even more recruitment centres were required to make it easier for the men to join up, but these locations are simply an overview of enlistment throughout London as a whole and not just within the confines of the City.

Before the war began in 1914 the British army had a total strength of some 710,000 men. Of this figure 247,432 were regular troops, full time soldiers already serving in His Majesty's Army, with another 300,000 in the Reserve. By the end of the war over five million men had enlisted in the British Army. About half of this number were volunteers, with the other half being conscripts. There was also what was known as the Derby Scheme, which was the brain child of Edward Stanley, 17th Earl of Derby and was brought in to effect in 1915. This was where men voluntarily registered their names for military service on the understanding that they would then only be called up when and if it was deemed necessary. 215,000 men enlisted this way, whilst another 2,185,000 attested for later enlistment.

In the early months of the war what became fondly known as Pals Battalions were formed all over the country. It was a simple yet effective way of getting men to join up. The hook was that a man would be able to join up, train and serve alongside his friends, relatives, work colleagues and his neighbours, rather than simply being allocated to whichever Regiment needed men the most at the time of their enlistment.

General Sir Henry Rawlinson, who at the beginning of the war was the General Officer Commanding 4th Division in France, knew only too well the importance of having large numbers of men available to fight in a war and it was he who came up with the idea of Pals Battalions. He was an experienced soldier, having passed out from the Royal Military College at Sandhurst in 1884 and posted as a lieutenant in the King's Own Royal Rifle Corps in India where he arrived on 6 February 1884. He served in Sudan in 1898 as a captain. He served with distinction during the Boer War in South Africa from 1899 to 1902, by which time he had reached the rank of lieutenant-colonel. He was a Londoner, born in Westminster, on 20 February 1864 and his Pals Battalions were a popular idea; by the end of 1916, approximately 750 Pals battalions had been raised.

With the introduction of conscription in January 1916 the idea appeared to have run its course. The Battle of the Somme brought home the very real problem with Pals battalions. It meant that when they went into battle and suffered heavy casualties, their communities back home also suffered terribly. In some towns and villages large numbers of men folk were killed which meant that some family names were lost forever. A sad example of this was the Accrington Pals, or the 11th (Service Battalion), East Lancashire Regiment, who were involved in the fighting on the first day of the Battle of the Somme. Out of a battalion strength of 700 men, 235 were killed with another 350 wounded, within the first twenty minutes of the battle.

In the summer of 1915 the first steps towards conscription began, almost unnoticed, with the National Registration Act. Men received a pink card that had to be completed and returned to the authorities so that they would know exactly how many they could call up when conscription eventually became law.

The Military Service Act 1916 was the first time that conscription had ever been used in British military history. The Bill which would eventually become the Act was first introduced by the then prime minister, Herbert Asquith in January 1916 and after being accepted into

Recruits swearing their allegiance to King George V.

law it came in to being on 2 March 1916. Before this the British government had relied on men enlisting in the Army of their own free will. Although conscription was introduced into Britain and New Zealand in 1916 and Canada in 1917, it was never actually introduced in Australia.

At the start of the First World War there were an estimated 300,000 Jews living throughout the country, most of whom had either arrived from Russia in the 1870s, or were their immediate descendants. Some of them wanted to fight for their adopted country, but for some, fighting in a war on the same side as Russia, the very country they had fled from to escape persecution, didn't sit so well. Under the terms of the Army Act as it stood at that time, foreign nationals were not allowed to enlist in the British Army as fighting troops.

Anti-Semitism did exist in pre-war Britain and some Jews were simply turned away when they tried to enlist. Some decided to put their religion down as Christian, because it was less aggravation and made it more likely that they would be accepted. Once the matter was brought to the attention of the British authorities they decided to act, and proactively dealt with the matter, coming up with recruitment posters specifically aimed at Jews.

'FRIENDLY ALIENS And the BRITISH ARMY
FRIENDLY ALIENS can now ENLIST in the British Army, and on the same terms as British-born Subjects.
All Aliens of Military Age who have resided for some time in this Country and are anxious to help should go to their Local Recruiting Office.
The Recruiting Officer will tell them what they must do and will help them to select their regiment if found fit.
Russian subject of the Jewish Faith can either apply at their own Recruiting Office or go to NEW COURT, ST. SWITHIN'S LANE EC.
The Jewish War Services Committee will help them into the Army and will send them to a Regiment where they have friends
DO NOT HESITATE BUT COME
AT ONCE AND DO YOUR DUTY
TO THE COUNTRY WHERE YOU
CHOSE TO RESIDE'

Jewish soldiers of the 38th Battalion Royal Fusiliers marching through London on 22 February 1918.

New Court, St Swithin's in the City of London was the location where a Jewish Battalion of the Royal Fusiliers was raised in August 1917, made up solely of Jewish men, creating the first of the Jewish Battalions, or the Jewish Legion as they were also unofficially called. The 38th Battalion was made up of British Jews and those men who had previously served with the Zion Mule Corps during the Gallipoli campaign. The 39th Battalion was raised at Fort Edward in Novia Scotia, Canada, and consisted of American and Canadian Jewish men who were resident in those countries. The 40th Battalion consisted of Palestinian Jews as well as a group of ninety-two Ottoman Jews who had been captured during the fighting at Gallipoli and then allowed to fight for the Allies. Ironically the 38th Battalion would later fight against troops from the Ottoman Empire in fighting north of Jerusalem. The other two Battalions, the 41st and 42nd were both depot Battalions stationed at Plymouth.

All of the men from the Battalions who survived the war were demobilized as soon as the Armistice had been signed. Ninety-one of them had been killed or died as a result of the war, with the 38th

Battalion losing the most men with forty-three. The only one of the Battalions not to lose any men was the 41st Battalion.

It wasn't just the Royal Fusiliers who had Jewish soldiers amongst their ranks, there were also Jews in the: Royal Air Force; Royal Artillery; London Regiment; Army Service Corps; Royal Engineers; Machine Gun Corps; Middlesex Regiment; Manchester Regiment; Tank Corps.

Before conscription was brought in, an estimated 10,000 Jewish men had voluntarily enlisted in the British Armed Forces, and by the end of the war the total number of British Jews who had served, had risen to 41,000.

The Military Service Act related to all men between the ages of eighteen and forty-one, meaning that they could all be called up for military service by the government as and when they saw fit. The only exceptions to this rule were if a man was married, was widowed with children, was serving in the Royal Navy (which of course was already military service), a religious minister, or somebody who was working in what had already been classified by the government as a reserved occupation, which meant that the job they were doing was deemed to be directly supporting the country's war effort.

Men were also entitled to claim that they were conscientious objectors and did not want to undertake military service, although in the eyes of most people they were seen as cowards who simply didn't have the backbone or moral fibre to fight for their country. By the end of the war, some 16,000 men had claimed the exemption of being a conscientious objector, which would then mean having to sit before a Military Service Tribunal, so that their claim could be assessed for its validity. These tribunals were intended to be fair and unbiased, but it was ultimately down to local councils and authorities to decide who would sit on their panels. They usually picked local businessmen, people with legal backgrounds and retired soldiers who had one thing in common; they were fiercely patriotic individuals who believed in their king and country and struggled to come to terms with why anybody might not be of the same mind.

Conscientious objectors were split into three distinct groups. There were the Absolutists, who in essence were opposed to conscription and war. Then there were the Alternatives, who were prepared to carry out alternative civilian work that was not under military control, and then there were Non-combatants, who were prepared to accept being called up in to the Army, but who did not want to be trained in the use of any kind of firearms. Non-combatants wore a uniform and were subject to army discipline and were basically used to provide physical labour. Some elements of the press liked to refer to them as the, 'No Courage Corps'

It could be argued that conscientious objectors weren't cowards at all but very brave individuals who had taken a stance on not participating in a war, knowing full well that in doing so, there would be elements of society who disliked, despised or even hated them for not fighting, and that forever more there would be a stain on their character and good name, possibly for the rest of their lives. But despite of all of this, they stuck to their principles. Some men had staunch religious beliefs which genuinely prevented them from fighting on moral grounds and wanted absolutely nothing to do with war and killing.

The following article appeared in the *Daily Mirror* on 25 March 1916 concerning Military Service Tribunals.

Tips for Tribunals
War Office help in choosing men for the fighting forces.

'Tribunals throughout the country will today receive an important circular from the War Office giving the following points for guidance:
- Requests for rehearing of cases to be granted. Inadequate grounds to be put plainly for appeal courts.
- Precise date of exemption on certificates.
- National service of conscientious cases to be decided by new committee.
- Tolerance and impartiality to be carefully observed.
- Quakers desire for service in Friends Ambulance Unit not to be contested.
- All tribunal hearings must not be taken in private.
- Industry and commerce to be carefully regarded where economical value is out of all proportion to military gain.
- Reasonable extension of time for conscripts appeals, having regard to urgent needs of Army for men.'

It is clear to see from this just how much of a sensitive topic conscientious objectors were to the government. They wanted to be seen to be doing the right thing, especially as this was a totally new phenomenon for them, which had come along on the back of conscription, an issue which they had obviously not even considered previously as a possibility.

The case of Francis Meynell, a conscientious objector, who sat before a Military Service Tribunal at Spring Gardens in London, was reported in the *Daily Herald* on Saturday 23 September 1916.

The Case of Francis Meynell

'Last week our friend and comrade Francis Meynell was before the appeal tribunal at Spring Gardens, London. He made a splendid and courageous stand for his claim to full and unconditional exemption. The tribunal was scrupulously fair and gave his case a full seventy minutes' discussion and consideration; but, while agreeing that he had proved his conscientious objection to all service, refused him exemption and ordered him to find work of national importance within twenty-eight days and further promised to consider an application for the right of appeal to the Central Tribunal. The case of our comrade illustrates the absurdity of the position with regard to the Military Service Act. This Act professedly gives the conscientious objector the right to claim exemption from military service on his being able to prove that he is possessed of a conscience to the satisfaction of the tribunals, but it leaves to the tribunal a discretion by which they can attach such conditions to their certificates of exemption as make it impossible for the out and out conscientious objectors to accept the exemption. Two thousand two hundred and sixty men have been arrested under the Conscription Acts; 1,266 have been court-martialled and 147 released.'

That article showed just how confusing the Military Service Act could be and more importantly how varied it could be in its interpretation, but with one member of the panel always having a military connection, the system was always going to be a difficult one to try and obtain a full exemption from having to undertake military service, no matter who was sitting on the three man panel.

Military Service Act, 1916.

 Only two months later in May 1916 the Act was amended to include married men. In 1918 the Act was amended for a third time which increased the upper age limit to fifty-one. The British Government had originally said that no men under the age of nineteen would be sent overseas to fight, but in April 1918 the age was lowered to eighteen, mainly because of the heavy losses that were still being incurred in the fighting on the Western Front.

A man, or his employer on his behalf, could apply to a local Military Service Tribunal that was sitting in the City of London, for a certificate of exemption to prevent him from being called up; where such exemptions were permitted they were usually either conditional or of a temporary nature. If not happy with the decision of the Military Service Tribunal there remained a right of appeal to the County Appeal Tribunal.

Another issue which isn't widely discussed when it comes to recruitment, is the degree of apathy which prevailed around the matter amongst certain groups of young working men, 40% of whom were over the age of twenty-one but were denied the right to vote. Some had no desire to fight for a country that didn't allow them to vote and elect the very people who had ultimately dragged the country into the war, and who were now determining that they should go off and fight in a war that they had absolute no interest in.

After the war the government instructed all local authorities to destroy all paperwork relating to Military Service Tribunals. Most authorities did as requested, but from a historical perspective, thankfully not all of them did, with some still surviving today in archives and Public Record Offices, notably a certain amount from Middlesex.

During the First World War, although Ireland was part of the United Kingdom, the Military Service Act did not, for purely political reasons, apply there.

There were other issues with recruitment which reduced the number of men who were willing to enlist. It has been estimated that in the region of 40% of all men who volunteered to join the armed forces were rejected as being unfit for military service on medical grounds. There were 1.5 million men who could not be called upon as they were working in what had been deemed to be essential occupations. In the City of London, this included being one of the Lord Mayors servants, making this a very sought after position.

The very first Lord Mayor of the City of London was Henry Fitz-Ailwin de Londonestone, who actually served in the role for an incredible twenty-three years, from 1189 until 19 September 1212, his reign only coming to an end because of his death at what was believed

The Lord Mayor of the City of London's servants.

to be the age of seventy-seven. He started his tenure at what was a difficult time politically. Richard I was at logger heads with the City of London over his desire and need to raise taxes, in the main to pay for the cost of his foreign wars. Richard would also go as far as to take out loans from some of London's wealthy merchants. In return for their co-operation, the merchants were given a large amount of power and freedom which allowed them to in effect rule themselves. This in turn led directly to the creation of the role of the Lord Mayor of the City of London. Prior to this the City of London, the aldermen and merchants came under the control of an officer of the crown, an individual who would have been appointed by the king.

By the time of the outbreak of the First World War, the position of the Lord Mayor of the City of London had long been a public position which was only held for a one year term of office. There was a particular process involved which went with becoming the Lord Mayor, which meant that only men of a certain standing, position or class, were ever going to be in a position to be even considered for the role.

There were five men who held this post during the First World War.

At the outbreak the Lord Mayor of London was Sir Thomas Vansittart Bowater who later went on to become a Conservative MP for the City of London between 1924 and 1938. He had previously held the position of the Sheriff of the City of London between 1905 and 1906, the latter being the year he was knighted by Edward VII.

Sir Thomas gave the following address soon after the war had begun.

'Keep your heads. There is no need for panic. Try and go on in the ordinary way. It is however necessary to exercise economy for the good of the community; and above and beyond, render such assistance as lies in your power to those poorer than yourselves. All who can should offer their services to the nation in whatever capacity is open and acceptable.'

Sir Thomas Vansittart Bowater, Lord Mayor of London at the outbreak of the war.

When he finished his year long stint as the Lord Mayor of the City of London he became Baronet Bowater of Hill Crest in Croydon. He was awarded numerous different honours during his life time including that of Honorary Colonel of the 10th Royal Fusiliers. He was also liked on the international stage, receiving honours from countries including two from Belgium, and one each from Denmark, France, Greece and Norway, from whom he received the Knight 1st Class of the Order of St Olaf.

As Thomas Vansittart Bowater finished his year in office as the Lord Mayor of the City as the First World War was about to begin, so his younger brother, Frank Henry Bowater, finished his year in office as Lord Mayor at the outbreak of the Second World War, serving his year in office between 1938 to 1939. Frank had been commissioned in to the 4th London Howitzer Brigade, which was a Territorial Unit, in 1905 and in 1908 he was promoted to the rank of major and he went on to serve in the First World War at the age of forty-eight.

1914 – Colonel Sir Charles Johnston

Before becoming the Lord Mayor of the City of London, Sir Charles had also been the Sheriff of the City of London in 1913, so he was well aware of the history, pomp and ceremony of the office he was about to embark on. He was elected to succeed Sir Thomas as the Lord Mayor on 29 September 1914, with the war not even two months old. His year in office began on Monday 9 November 1914, when he left the Guildhall and marched to the nearby Law Courts to take the oath of the office of Lord Mayor of the City of London and for the Lord Chief Justice to express the king's approval of his appointment.

Colonel Sir Charles Johnston in his official robes of office.

Colonel Sir Charles Johnston in less formal attire.

The procession, which left from the Guildhall at 1 pm, was led by a detachment of soldiers from the king's overseas dominion regiment, followed by some 300 members of the Naval Volunteer Reserve.

In attendance were over 2000 troops from Canadian, New Zealand, and New Foundland regiments; both cavalry units as well as infantry were represented. Other regiments that were part of the procession included the Royal Marines, the London Scottish Regiment, the King Edward's Horse, Royal Naval Division boys from the *Warspite* and the Seaman's Orphanage. Various Yeomanry regiments, including the

*The Lord Mayors Parade
Monday 9 November
1914.*

*The Royal Naval Division
marching through London.*

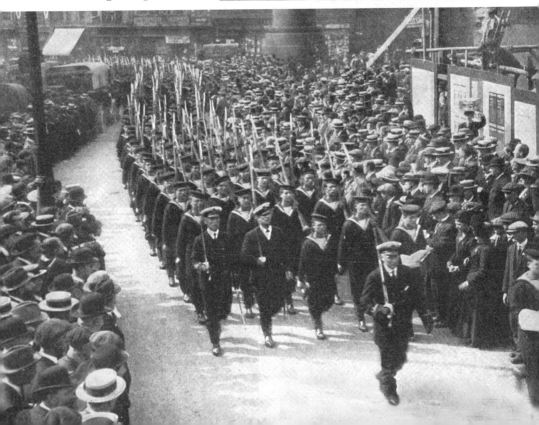

Rough Riders and Dragoons, the Royal Field and Garrison Artillery, the Rifle Brigade, the Red Cross and the Officers Training Corps also took part.

The procession included a total of six military bands from the Naval Division, the Honorary Artillery Company, the Coldstream Guards, the Corps of Commissionaires, the 5th Battalion, Royal Sussex Regiment and the Band of the Royal Horse Guards.

With no rain, just sunshine on a crisp, cold day, the crowds, who were out in their thousands, lined the route, clapping and cheering enthusiastically as the procession passed by, the most advantageous location on the route being the steps of St Paul's Cathedral, which had been occupied by densely packed crowds hours before the occasion began. It was a memorable day, full of splendour, and military might, which was appropriate to both the occasion and the circumstances of being at war.

What was noticeable by their absence were banners, streamers, garlands and Venetian poles, none of which were displayed to any great degree, with the only real touch of colour coming from the flags of England and her Allies that were fluttering gently in the morning breeze.

Many visitors found the lack of colour so confusing that there were repeated occasions when they were seen asking supporting Police officers if they were in the right street for the Lord Mayor's procession.

This was possibly the first chance the public had had of seeing a large military procession in such positive circumstances since the war had begun. Besides the occasion being a massive morale booster for members of the public, the authorities were secretly hoping that it would also provide a much needed boost to the nation's recruitment drive for more men to enlist in the Armed forces. The procession's direct style and appearance found an echo in the streets which it passed through. Business as usual was the clear message coming from the City of London on this momentous occasion. The event was described in the newspapers the following day.

'Though the procession lacked the brilliant colour to which Londoners have become so accustomed it was never the less the most inspiring spectacle seen in the city for many years. A few short weeks of training had given the young men composing the

Mansion House, the Lord Mayors official residence.

Sir Charles Johnston is third from the left. The man on the far left of the photograph is Sir William Dunn, who was the Lord Mayor of the City of London at the time of the photograph. The man next to him is, Sir William Treloar, and the man on the far right of the photograph is Sheriff Touche. The photograph was taken in Harrogate, Yorkshire. (Daily Mirror 21 August 1916)

various units a martial bearing which made it difficult to believe that they had so recently taken from the counting house, the office, the factory or the field. There were remarkable scenes of enthusiasm as they swung through the city streets.'

With the war in its infancy, Sir Charles's year in office would have been a memorable one for sure, a year in which 148,019 Commonwealth soldiers were killed or died from their wounds, illness or disease, with more than double that amount being wounded.

1915 – Colonel Sir Charles Wakefield

Sir Charles was born on 12 December 1859 in Liverpool on Merseyside and was educated at the Liverpool Institute. He went on to become a successful business man who made his fortune out of patenting the Wakefield Lubricator for steam engines, which would also go on to be used for aeroplanes. motorcycles and cars.

Sir Charles's year as the Mayor of the City of London coincided with the first full year of the war, this was a time which saw a total of 151,285 Commonwealth servicemen die.

He took an active interest in the country's young men who had enlisted and were fighting in the war. On 12 August 1915 he arranged

Colonel Sir Charles Wakefield – Hampton Court 12 August 1915.

Colonel Sir Charles Wakefield in his ceremonial robes.

for 1,000 wounded and convalescing men from hospitals in and around London to visit a specially arranged fete at Hampton Court. The day was a success and one that was thoroughly enjoyed by the men, who happily participated in the amusements that were provided. They particularly liked the competition which took place between the Lord Mayor, in all of his civil dignitary attire, including his robes, feathered hat and chains of office, and General MacKintosh, in full military uniform and in possession of his dress sword, in a game at the cocoa nut shy stall, with neither man holding back.

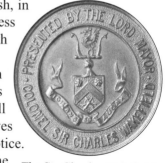

Sir Charles had previously been to the Western Front to see for himself the trials and tribulations the men had to endure on a daily basis, whilst still being fresh and alert enough to fight for their lives against their German foes, often at a moment's notice.

On the night of 31 March/1 April 1916, the German Zeppelin L15 was brought down in the sea off of Margate, close to the Kentish Knock

The Sir Charles Wakefield Medal.

lightship. Sir Charles had originally offered a substantial financial reward for the first anti-aircraft units to shoot down a German Zeppelin, but because so many different units claimed they had been the ones responsible for bringing down the aircraft it was difficult to clearly establish who had actually been responsible for firing the decisive shots. In the circumstances Sir Charles rewarded each of the anti-aircraft and search light batteries involved. This meant purchasing and providing a total of 300 medals, each of which was made out of 8 carat gold.

2nd Lieutenant Alfred de Bathe Brandon, a New Zealand pilot and a member of the Royal Flying Corps, who was flying a B E 2e fighter plane, and the first to engage the Zeppelin, was awarded a Military Cross for his part in the bringing down of the airship.

Prior to becoming the Lord Mayor of the City of London, Sir Charles had previously been an Alderman of the City, and the Sheriff of London in 1907. His subsequent honours after having being Knighted for services to the City of London, were when he became Baron Wakefield of Hythe in 1930 and in 1934, when he was made Viscount Wakefield of Hythe.

1916 – Sir William Henry Dunn (Baronet)

Sir William Henry Dunn was born in Clitheroe, Lancaster on 8 October 1856. He was both a surveyor and an auctioneer by profession, working extensively in the City of London. Like his predecessor, Sir Charles Wakefield, he had also been an Alderman and a Sheriff of the City of London, the latter, a position he filled in 1906, the year before Sir

Sir William Henry Dunn in his official robes.

Charles Wakefield had held the same position. He was knighted the following year in 1907. He was also a Conservative Member of Parliament, albeit for less than a year, when he won the seat for Southwark West from the sitting Liberal MP, Richard Causton, in the General Election of 15 January 1910. He lost the seat when there was a further General Election on 28 November of that year, when he was ousted by the new Liberal MP, Edward Anthony Strauss. Sir William was famous – or perhaps infamous – for asking just one question during his time as MP, regarding the conditions of a post office rest room.

1917 – Sir Charles Augustine Hanson (1st Baronet)

Sir Charles was a truly remarkable man who lived a varied yet interesting life. His success in life had come through both the financial world as well as that of politics, the foundations of which were laid in Canada, before returning to England and his home county of Cornwall. Whilst in Canada he established the firm of Hanson Brothers in Montreal, one of the largest firms of private bankers in the country. Prior to becoming the Lord Mayor of the City of London in 1917, he had been an Alderman in 1909 as well as the Sheriff of London in 1911 for a year. After his term of office as the Lord Mayor he became an MP for South-East Cornwall, representing the Cornwall Unionists Party.

Sir Charles Augustine Hanson in his official robes.

1918 – Colonel Sir Horace Brooks Marshall

Sir Horace's year of tenure as Lord Mayor of the City of London was 1918-1919. He was a well-educated man who was born in Streatham, a suburb of London, on 5 August 1865. After attending both Dulwich College and Trinity College in Dublin, he started work at his father's newspaper business in Fleet Street, London. Horace Brooks Marshall, senior, had revolutionised the sales of both books and magazines on the railways, which greatly added to his personal fortune. He received his knighthood in 1902 when he was thirty-seven years of age, on the occasion of Edward VII's coronation. Before becoming the Lord Mayor he had fulfilled numerous different public positions of note, including Sheriff of the City of London, in 1902. This role in particular was one that custom dictated had to have been held before a person could be considered for the higher position of Lord Mayor of the City of London.

Sir Horace was still in his year of office when the First World War ended and as such was a prominent individual in the City's victory celebrations.

CHAPTER 3

The Bank of England

During the First World War the Bank of England was part of the very fabric of British society that collectively formed the heartbeat of the nation, the back bone of what made the country what it was, a major power on the world stage. Along with Buckingham Palace, the Houses of Parliament and the Tower of London, the Bank of England was part of the epicentre of what made the country tick and helped drive it forward in its hour of need.

With George V being the monarch as well as the head of the armed forces, the connection between the nations four main institutions, of political, financial, military and royalty, were intrinsically linked. Add to this the estimated cost of the war to the British Government running

The Bank of England 1915. (From the Bank of England Archive)

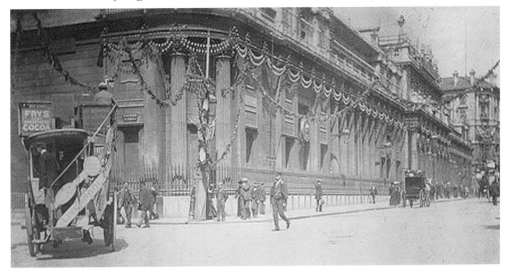

King George V and Queen Mary printing the first national war bond in the printing department at the Bank of England. (Bank of England Archive)

at an estimated £6 million a day and it was easy to see just how much each of them relied upon each other to survive.

The Bank of England not only oversaw and protected the nation's monetary and gold reserves during the war, but helped to sustain financial stability and keep the nation afloat; resulting in gold sovereigns and half-sovereigns being withdrawn from circulation and replaced with bank notes. It also provided man power for the armed forces, as during the course of the war over 400 members of the Bank of England staff enlisted in His Majesty's armed forces. Sadly not all of them came back; seventy-one members of staff were either killed in action or died of their wounds during the war.

At the beginning of the First World War there were some 1300 people, the vast majority of whom were men (only 66 women), working at the Bank of England at Threadneedle Street; but that number of staff was very quickly depleted when 414 of the Bank's staff left to go off and fight in the war. The war brought with it a lot of extra work for the staff of the Bank, the numbers of staff needed to be increased and men understandably were at a premium. Men of a certain age who were physically fit and healthy were going to be called up at some time and with this in mind the Bank took on 2,400 women during the war.

The Bank of England's Roll of Honour commemorates the names of its members of staff who served in the Great War. Those who were killed have a cross along with the first letter or their surname etched in gold. The photographs of the four tablets are taken from the Bank of England Archive. The Memorial, which was unveiled on 11 November 1921 and was dedicated by the Rev. E E Holmes (Archdeacon) has the following inscription.

'To the Comrades who, at duty's
call, crossed the
Dark waters to the further shore
1914-1919.'

1914 — 1918.

JOHNSON V A · ✝ JONES E · KEEBLE C H
KENNEDY C A R · KIDD J C · KIDD R C
KIDDLE H D · KING D J · KING R G
KNOLLYS F E · ✝ LACK J W · LANDON E C T
LANGSTON CLARENCE · LAVINGTON D P
LAW H S · LAWFORD WINGATE
LEFFLER HEREWARD · LEVANDER H J
LEWIS F A · LIDINGTON H V
✝ LINFORD I H · ✝ LINK O L E · LITTLE H A K
LODGE A T · LONG A L D · ✝ LOVELOCK H W
LOVETT G F · LOWRY M W · LUXON E C
MCANALLY J A · MACBEAN C A
MACDERMOTT E J · MACKAY DONALD
MACKENZIE A D · MACKENZIE D M · MANBY R L
✝ MARCHMENT W J · MARRIOTT H J B
MARSHALL HENRY · ✝ MARTIN E J
MARTIN THOMAS · MASON JOHN
MAULE W H F · ✝ MAUNSELL R H P
MAYER P W W · MEADE W C A · MELDRUM R F A
✝ MERTENS H G · ✝ MICHELL A C · MILES C R W
MILES MAURICE · MILLER H C
MOLYNEUX H B · MOMBRUN JAMES
MORSHEAD V H · MOUNT EDWARD
MURPHY F F · MURRAY W T · NAIRNE F M
NASH C G · NASH GEORGE · ✝ NASH H M
NASH T · NEPEAN E C Y ST V · NEVILL W H
NEWMAN C F · NEWMAN H A A · NICHOLSON J W
NOBBS J H B · ✝ NOEL F M · OWEN JOHN
OXENBOULD B H · ✝ PAGE B C · PAGE H N
✝ PALFREYMAN G A · PEARCE CUTHBERT
PEARL G W · PEPPIATT K O · PERCEVAL F C C G
PETHERBRIDGE R C · PHILLIPS G C
PHILLIPS H G E · PHILPOTT W H · PITMAN A T
PIZZEY ALBERT · POLGREEN J C V
POWELL F F J · PRATT F G · PURCHAS G J
✝ PURDIE F P · ✝ PURTON G L · RANFT R C
REDFERN NORMAN · REID J C A
RENDALL HERBERT · REYNOLDS E J

Bank of England Roll of Honour.

Sadly, some of the men whose names appear are not traceable, but many have well-attested military details and a selection follows:

Lionel Edward Allen was thirty-two years of age and a private (766372) in the 1st/28th Battalion, London Regiment (Artists' Rifles) when he died of his wounds (received in fighting on 31 December 1917) on 2 January 1918. He is buried at the Rocquigny-Equancourt

Road, British Cemetery at Mannancourt which is in the Somme region of France.

Before the war Lionel had worked as a Bank Clerk at the Bank of England in the City of London.

Geoffrey Walter Henry Applin was a second lieutenant in the 1st Battalion, Lincolnshire Regiment when he was killed in action on 1 July 1916, on the very first day of the Battle of the Somme. Commonwealth forces, numbering thirteen divisions, launched an attack on German lines between Gommecourt and Maricourt. The British casualties for the first day alone were an estimated 50,000, of which 20,000 were killed. The infantry attack had been proceeded by an Allied artillery bombardment of the German lines which had lasted for a week, but despite this the German defences remained largely in place. The expected unopposed ground attack was instead met with a ferocious defensive action which saw German machine gun units have a field day. It remains as the biggest loss of casualties on a single day in British military history. Lieutenant Applin's body was never found and he has no known grave. His name is commemorated on the Thiepval Memorial which is located in the Somme region of France.

Stanley Jerram Atkinson was a private (536930) in the 13th (Kennsington) Battalion, London Regiment when he died on 30 December 1917. He was on board the vessel SS *Aragon*, a troop ship that had just arrived at the port of Alexandria in Egypt, having left Marseilles on 17 December, with 2,700 officers and men bound for the fighting in Palestine. Initially she was allowed to enter the harbour, which for all shipping was a safe environment, but for some unknown reason she was then instructed to wait outside the harbour and to drop her anchor, still with her crew and cargo of troops. She was attacked by the German submarine *UC-34*. A total of 380 Commonwealth officers and men, including Stanley, were drowned when the ship sank after having being torpedoed.

His body was never recovered and his name is commemorated on the Chatby Memorial in Egypt. The incident was made even worst when HMS *Attack* who rushed to the scene to pick up survivors from the *Aragon* was also torpedoed by the same submarine.

SS Aragon.(www.wrecksite.eu)

Chatby Memorial Egypt. (Commonwealth War Graves Commission)

Harry Edward Benstead was a twenty-four year old second lieutenant in the 7th Battalion, London Regiment but attached to the 1st/5th Battalion London Regiment (London Rifle Brigade), when he was killed in action on 14 April 1917. He is buried at the Wancourt British Cemetery in the Pas de Calais region of France.

William Rushbury Berrow was a private (91863) in 'E' Battalion, Tank Corps, when he was killed on 23 November 1917 at the Battle of Cambrai. His name is commemorated on the Cambrai Memorial, which is situated in the Nord region of France. This was the battle that saw tanks used for the first time on such a large scale. The battle was also memorable for British senior officers deciding to halt the offensive after two days to allow for 'rest and reorganisation.' The Germans took full advantage of this break by bringing up reinforcements.

Ernest Alexander Boyer was a twenty-eight year old second lieutenant in the 7th Battalion, London Regiment attached to the 1st/22nd Battalion of the same Regiment, when he was killed in action on 5 April 1918 during the Arras offensive. His name is commemorated on the Arras Memorial in the Pas de Calais region of France.

Arras Memorial (Commonwealth War Graves Commission)

Ramleh War Cemetery (Commonwealth War Graves Commission)

Archibald Charles Watson Buck was a second lieutenant in the 10th Battalion (Liverpool Scottish), The King's (Liverpool Regiment), which was a Territorial Unit, when he was killed in action on 9 August 1916 during the early weeks of the Battle of the Somme. Initially he had been reported as being missing in action. His body was never recovered and his name is commemorated on the Thiepval Memorial.

Arthur Edward Adderley Buller was thirty-five years of age and a captain in the Inns of Court Officer Training Corps, but attached to the 1st/5th Battalion, Norfolk Regiment when he died of dysentery on 21 September 1918. He is buried at the Ramleh War Cemetery in Israel.

The 1911 Census showed Arthur living at number 5 Waldegrave Road, Strawberry Hill, Twickenham, Middlesex, with his mother, Gertrude, his two sisters, Hilda and Gertrude and his brother, Richard Francis Montague Buller, who like Arthur, was a Clerk at the Bank of England.

Richard Francis Montague Buller was thirty-three years of age and a major in the 7th Battalion, (Duke of Cambridge's Own) Middlesex Regiment and was attached to the 8th Battalion of the same Regiment when he was killed in action on 24 August 1918 at Croisilles in France, dying a month before his elder brother, Arthur. He has no known grave and his name is commemorated on the Vis-en-Artois Memorial. The 8th Battalion were involved in the heavy fighting to retake Croisilles which had been lost to the Germans on 21 March 1918. It was finally recaptured on 28 August 1918, four days after Richard was killed.

Poor widowed Mrs Gertrude Buller had not only experienced the pain of losing both of her sons in the war but she had lost them both within a month of each other. The sadness of her loss can only be guessed at.

Jas. R T Burrow was thirty-four years of age and a Rifleman (S/19794) in the 2nd Battalion, Rifle Brigade when he was killed in action on 8 March 1917. He is buried at the Bray Military Cemetery in the Somme region of France.

The village of Bray-sur-Somme was, throughout 1916 and 1917, used as both a main dressing station and casualty clearing station, but the

Bray Military Cemetery. (Commonwealth War Graves Commission)

Gouzeacourt New British Cemetery. (Commonwealth War Graves Commission)

village fell into German hands during the first few days of March 1918 and it was during this fighting that Rifleman Burrow was killed.

Frederick William Cheswick was a thirty-five year old rifleman (S/26595) with the 2nd Battalion, Rifle Brigade when he was killed in action on 21 April 1917. He is buried in Gouzeaucourt New British Cemetery.

Cyril John Digby Clarke was a second lieutenant in the South Midland Company, Army Service Corps when he was killed on 15 September 1917. He is buried at the Vlamertinghe New Military Cemetery, which is situated in the West-Vlaanderen region of Belgium. The 3rd Battle of Ypres, 31 July to 10 November 1917, was going on at the time of Cyril's death, in the area where he is buried, so it is more than likely he was killed during the battle.

Herbert Clement was twenty-nine years of age, a Captain in the 3rd Battalion, Royal Warwickshire Regiment, who was attached to the 14th Battalion of the same regiment. which Besides being a Service Battalion, it was also known as the 1st Birmingham Pals. He was killed

Doullens Communal Cemetery Extension No.1 (Commonwealth War Graves Commission)

in action on 10 October 1917 during fighting in the Third Battle of Ypres. He has no known grave and his name is commemorated on the Tyne Cot Memorial, in the West-Vlaanderen region of Belgium.

Vernon Swann Crosier was twenty-four years of age and a second lieutenant in the 7th Battalion, London Regiment when he died of his wounds on 6 April 1918 during the German spring offensive. He had previously been a private (8163/762201) in the Regiments 28th Battalion. He is buried at the Doullens Communal Cemetery Extension No. 1.

Prior to the war Vernon Crosier had been a Clerk working at the Bank of England in the City of London.

Robert Hammond Cunningham was thirty-two years of age and a private (205342) in the 2nd Battalion, York and Lancaster Regiment when he was killed in action on 18 September 1918 during heavy fighting at the village of Holnon and the nearby woods, with German forces, between 14 and 19 September 1918. He is buried in the Chapelle British Cemetery, Holnon which is situated in the Aisne region of France. Before being in the 2nd Battalion, York & Lancaster Regiment, Robert had been in 2nd/4th Battalion and the 13th Battalion of the same regiment and before that he had been Private 3235, 2nd Company, London Yeomanry, originally enlisting on 9 December 1915. He had also at some time being a gunner in the Tank Corps. He arrived at the base camp at Etaples in France on 1 November 1917. He had already been posted to the 2nd Battalion, York & Lancaster Regiment when he was reported as wounded and missing on 18 September 1918.

John Darker was an Able Seaman (J/47737) in the Royal Navy working on board HMS *Simoon* when he was killed in action on 23 January 1917. HMS *Simoon* was a Royal Navy R Class Destroyer which was part of the Harwich Force when she was struck by a torpedo fired by the German Destroyer *S 50*, off Schouwen on the Belgium coast, which caused her magazine to explode. Forty-seven out of a crew of ninety, including John Darker, perished. Their bodies were never recovered and their names are commemorated on the Chatham Naval Memorial.

Bank of England Roll of Honour.

Harold H Dawes was a private (8352 + 762365) in the 1st/28th Battalion, London Regiment (Artists' Rifles) when he was killed in action on 30 October 1917 whilst fighting during the Second Battle of Passchendaele. He has no known grave and his name is commemorated on the Tyne Cot Memorial in Belgium.

Clifford Mostyn French Dewdney was born on 7 June 1896 in Merthyr Tydfil, Glamorgan. He was educated at Plymouth College and Bromsgrove School, Worcester, before gaining a commission and becoming a second lieutenant in the Gloucestershire Regiment on 29 September 1915. He took part in the Battle of the Somme and was wounded on 20 August 1916 at Guillemont. He was promoted to lieutenant later that year on 16 December 1916. Two months after that on 20 February 1917 he was further promoted to Assistant Adjutant before becoming a captain on 15 April 1917, in the 14th Battalion, Gloucestershire Regiment, attached to the 7th Battalion, Queen's Own (Royal West Kent Regiment) when he was killed in action on 4 April 1918 at Hangard Wood. A fellow officer wrote of him, 'It was at Hangard Wood, near Villers Bretonneux, and his sacrifice practically saved our line from going completely.' There is an entry in the De Ruvigny's Roll of Honour, 1914-1919 for Clifford which outlines his achievements. He has no known grave and his name is commemorated on the Pozieres Memorial, in the Somme region of France. For his bravery, he was Mentioned in Despatches on 23 May 1918 by Field Marshal Sir Douglas Haig for 'gallant and distinguished service in the field', and was also awarded the French Croix de Guerre with star, for his exceptional services in the Flanders front in October 1917.

John Hastings Dinsmore was born in Coundon in County Durham on 8 September 1887. He was educated at Kelso High School and started working at the Bank of England in 1907. He obtained a commission as a second lieutenant with the 3rd Battalion (Reserve) The Buffs (East Kent Regiment) on 5 June 1915. He was wounded at the Battle of Hooge on 30 July 1915, which was a village near Ypres in Belgium, and sent back to England. The battle was remembered for the first major deployment of flame throwers by the Germans.

He would remain in England recuperating from his wounds for more than a year, during which time he had married Anita Johannes, the daughter of a retired Vice-Consol of Argentina. He returned to the Western Front on 14 September 1916, and was attached to The Buffs 6th Battalion. He was killed in action on 3 May 1917 whilst leading his men at Monchy-au-Bois during the Battle of Arras.

Thomas Mitchell Dow was twenty-seven years of age and a private (3473) in the 1st Battalion, Honourable Artillery Company, when he was killed in action on 10 February 1917. He is buried at the Etaples Military Cemetery, in the Pas de Calais region of France.

Etaples Military Cemetery (Commonwealth War Graves Commission)

Arnold Inman Draper was thirty-five years of age and a married man. He was a major in the 17th Battalion, The King's (Liverpool Regiment), having first arrived in France on 7 November 1915. He was killed in action on 21 October 1917 and is buried at the Kemmel Chateau Military Cemetery in the West-Vlaanderen region of Belgium.

George Richard Eddie was thirty-six years of age and a lieutenant in 1st/4th (Hallamshire) Battalion, York and Lancaster Regiment, which was a Territorial Unit, when he died of flu at Boulogne on 3 November 1918, just eight days from the signing of the Armistice. He is buried in the Terlincthun British Cemetery at Wimille, close to Boulogne in the Pas de Calais region of France. He had initially been a private (614) in the Honourable Artillery Company before receiving his commission, having initially arrived in France on 29 December 1914.

Kemmel Chateau Military Cemetery. (Commonwealth War Graves Commission)

Richard Guy Eric Galpin was thirty-eight years of age and a private (536940) in the 15th Battalion, London Regiment (Price of Wales' Own Civil Service Rifles) when he died on 30 December 1917. He has no known grave and his name is commemorated on the Chatsby Memorial in Egypt. He drowned when the Troopship he was on, SS *Aragon*, was hit by a torpedo at Alexandria Harbour in Egypt, fired from the German Submarine *UC-34*.

G H M Gameson was a second lieutenant in the 8th Battalion, Northumberland Fusiliers when he was killed on 14 March 1917, at the start of the German withdrawal of its troops from the battlefields of the Somme as they slowly began their retreat back to the Hindenburg Line, which went on until 5 April. This led to some fierce fighting in and around Bucquoy as Commonwealth forces wrestled the village from the clutches of the German defenders. It was during this fighting that Second Lieutenant Gameson was killed. He is buried at the Queens Cemetery, Bucquoy in the Pas de Calais region of France

Arthur R Garton was twenty-six years of age and a lieutenant in the 6th Battalion, Northumberland Fusiliers when he was killed in action on 26 April 1915. Prior to his death he had been mentioned in despatches for his bravery. He has no known grave and his name is commemorated on the Ypres (Menin Gate) Memorial in Belgium.

Joseph William Gevaux was twenty-nine years of age and a private (611937) in the 19th Battalion (St Pancras), London Regiment, which was a Territorial Unit. They had first arrived in France, landing at Le Havre, on 11 May 1915, becoming part of the 2nd London Division. Joseph was killed in action on 12 July 1917.

Ralph Gordon O'Connor Glynn was a private (4665) (302775) in the 2nd/5th Battalion (City of London), London Regiment (London Rifle Brigade). He was killed in action on 18 June 1917 but as his body was never found he has no known grave and his name is therefore commemorated on the Arras Memorial in the Pas de Calais region of France.

Donald Alfred Harnett was a second lieutenant in the 3rd Battalion, The Buffs (East Kent Regiment), attached to the 6th Battalion of the same Regiment, when he was killed in action on 7 October 1916. His name is commemorated on the Thiepval Memorial.

Frederick James Herbert was twenty-three years of age and a Rifleman (5647) (652517) in the 1st/21st Battalion (First Surrey Rifles) London Regiment, when he was killed in action on 8 October 1916. His name is also commemorated on the Thiepval Memorial. When he had initially enlisted in the Army he had joined the Oxford and Bucks Light Infantry as a private (21834), enlisting at Bletchley in Buckinghamshire, before later transferring to the London Regiment.

Thomas Edwin William Hewett was a twenty year old rifleman (1805) in the 6th Battalion (City of London Rifles) London Regiment, when he was killed in action on 25 September 1915. He is buried at the Maroc British Cemetery, near the village of Grenay, in the Pas de Calais region of France.

Peronne Communal Cemetery Extension. (Commonwealth War Graves Commission)

Robert Valentine Hodgson was twenty-two years of age when he was killed in action on 31 May 1918. He was a rifleman (608457) in the 18th Battalion (London Irish Rifles) London Regiment and is buried in the Peronne Communal Cemetery Extension in the Somme region of France.

When he had originally enlisted at Croydon in Surrey, he had been a private (302715) in the 5th Battalion, London Regiment. The war diaries for the 18th Battalion, London Regiment, show that on 31 May 1918 they were 'in the line' at Warloy in France, and that everything was 'quiet', but there is no action or battle recorded that would have likely resulted in Robert being wounded.

Sydney Hodson was twenty-seven years of age and a second lieutenant in the 5th Battalion, King's Royal Rifle Corps, although at the time of his death on 21 March 1918, he was attached to the Regiments 9th Battalion. He has no known grave and is commemorated on the Pozieres Memorial which is situated in the Somme Region of France.

William Frederick Houlding first arrived in France on 14 December

1915. Having enlisted at Chelsea in London, he became an Acting Corporal (GS/62144), in the 4th Battalion, Royal Fusiliers (City of London Regiment) and was killed in action on 9 April 1917 during fighting on the first day of the Battle of Arras. British troops, along with South African and other Commonwealth forces, attacked German defensive positions near the city of Arras, which although resulted in some initial gains on the first day, subsequently stalled with neither side gaining or losing any more ground.

William is buried at the Tilloy British Cemetery, Tilloy-les-Mofflaines, in the Pas de Calais region of France. Before the war William was a Clerk working at the Bank of England. He was a married man living at 152 Ravensbury Road, Wandsworth, London, with his wife Jane and their two year old son, also William.

Albert P Hudson was a twenty-six year old private (42480) in the 1st/10th Battalion, London Regiment, when he died of pneumonia on 19 January 1919. He is buried at the Alexandria (Hadra) War Memorial Cemetery, Egypt.

Meredith Charles Clifton James was born in Perth, Australia in 1895,

Tilloy British Cemetery. (Commonwealth War Graves Commission)

and originally enlisted as a private (1312) in the 28th (County of London) Battalion London Regiment (Artists Rifles). On 24 July 1915 he was commissioned in to the 1st Battalion, Worcestershire Regiment, as a second lieutenant. At the time of his death on 21 October 1916 he was twenty-two years of age. His battalion were holding front line trenches in the Gueudecourt area; it was bitterly cold to the point that keeping warm was the order of the day. As if inclement weather wasn't difficult enough to have to defend against, they came under a heavy and sustained German artillery attack. For the 1st Battalion this resulted in some fifty-two casualties, with eleven dead, thirty-eight wounded and three men missing who were presumed to be dead. One of the eleven who were confirmed as having been killed was Meredith James.

John Westlake Lack was a captain in the 8th Battalion, Suffolk Regiment when he died of his wounds on 26 July 1916, sustained during fighting in the early weeks of the Battle of the Somme. He is buried at Abbeville Communal Cemetery which is situated in the Somme region of France.

Bank of England Roll of Honour.

Before the war John Lack was single and an Insurance Clerk. His brother, Edward, also served in the war. He had enlisted on 1 September 1916 and became a private (493125) in the 13th (County of London) Battalion, London Regiment (Princess Louise's Kensington Rifles), finally being demobbed on 2 January 1919.

Harold William Lovelock was a regimental sergeant major (530438) in the 15th Battalion, (Prince of Wales Own Civil Service) London Regiment, which was a Territorial Unit, when he was killed in action on the Western Front on 28 September 1918. He had been awarded the

Abbeville Communal Cemetery. (Commonwealth War Graves Commission)

Meritorious Service Medal earlier in the war and is buried in the Bailleul Communal Cemetery Extension, in the Nord region of France.

Harold was a married man as well as a father and before the war he lived at number 66 Harvard Court, Honeybourne Road, West Hampstead, with his wife Isabel, who he had married in 1909, and their one year old son, Robert. Harold was a clerk at the Bank of England.

Before the war William James Marchment was a stockbroker's clerk. He was a lieutenant and acting in the rank of captain in 'X' Company, 32nd Trench Mortar Battery, Royal Field Artillery, when he was killed in action on 4 November 1918, a week before the end of the fighting and the signing of the Armistice. He is buried in the Highland Cemetery, at Le Cateau.

Edwin John Martin who was a second lieutenant in the 1st Battalion, London Regiment (Royal Fusiliers). He was twenty-six years of age and was killed in action on 4 September 1918, having only arrived in France a month earlier on 3 August, and is buried in the Wulverghem-Lindenhoek Road Military Cemetery, in the West-Vlaanderen region

Bailleul Communal Cemetery Extension, Nord. (Commonwealth War Graves Commission)

of Belgium. When Edwin's medals for his wartime service were sent to his wife in September 1920, she was living at number 18 Clifton Road, Church End, Finchley, London, N3.

Reginald Harcourt Proctor Maunsell was thirty-seven years of age and a second lieutenant in the 128th Siege Battalion, Royal Garrison Artillery, and was killed in action on 27 April 1918. He is buried at the Hagle Dump Cemetery near Leper in the West-Vlaanderen region of Belgium. After enlisting at Brighton, Hugh Grier Mertens became a private (495707) in the 13th (County of London) Battalion, London Regiment (Princess Louise's Kensington Rifles). He was killed in action on 9 August 1918, on the second day of the Battle of Amiens and is buried at the Beacon cemetery in the village of Sailly-Laurette. Remarkably, this part of the Somme region did not see any fighting until 26 March 1918, but the cemetery still contains the graves of 772 Commonwealth servicemen.

Arthur C Michell was a second lieutenant of the 7th Battalion, Queen's Own (Royal West Kent Regiment) who was killed in action on 12 October 1917, the first day of the First Battle of Passchendaele. He has no known grave and his name is commemorated on the Tyne Cott Memorial.

Herbert Maurice Nash was twenty-four years of age and a private (3094) in the 1st/15th Battalion, London Regiment (Prince of Wales Own Civil Service Rifles) when he was killed in action on 21 December 1915. He has no known grave and his name is commemorated on the Loos Memorial in the Pas de Calais region of France.

Herbert's younger brother, Frederick Lionel Nash, was also killed in the war. He was a Rifleman (3039) in the 12th (County of London) Battalion (The Rangers) when he was killed in action on 25 April 1915 aged just seventeen, officially not old enough to have actually been on active service. Like his brother, he has no known grave, His name is commemorated on the Ypres (Menin Gate) Memorial.

General Sir Cecil Frederick Nevil Macready, 1st Baronet, GCMB, KCB, had passed out from the Royal Military College, Sandhurst in October 1881 and was commissioned as a second lieutenant into the 1st Battalion, Gordon Highlanders. He served during the First World War, arriving in France with the British Expeditionary Force in 1915. In August 1918, he became the Commissioner of the Metropolitan Police in London, a position he remained in until April 1920 when he then became General Officer Commanding-in-Chief, British Forces in Ireland.

Beacon Cemetery, Sailly-Laurette. (Commonwealth War Graves Commission)

Francis Methuen Noel was a twenty-eight year old captain in the 4th Battalion but attached to the 9th Battalion, Devonshire Regiment, when he was killed in action on 26 October 1917. He has no known grave and his name is commemorated on the Tyne Cott Memorial.

B C Page was a married man. He and his wife, Wilhelmenia, lived at number 94 Lumley Buildings, Holbein Place, Sloane Street, London. He enlisted in the Army during the course of the war as private 612162 in the 2nd/19th (St Pancras) Battalion London Regiment and he was killed in action on 12 October 1918 during fighting with Ottoman forces. He is buried in the Ramleh War Cemetery in Israel

George Alexander Palfreyman was twenty-three years of age and before the war he was a clerk at the Bank of England in the City of London. During the war he became a second lieutenant in the 3rd Battalion, The Buffs (East Kent Regiment) attached to number 7 Squadron Royal Flying Corps. When he originally enlisted, he did so as a gunner (62449) in the Royal Garrison Artillery, before receiving a commission with The Buffs, arriving in France on 26 June 1916.

Arras Flying Services Memorial. (Commonwealth War Graves Commission)

His name is commemorated on the Arras Flying Services Memorial in the Pas de Calais region of France. When he was killed on 26 October 1916 it was whilst flying his aircraft high up in the sky rather than dashing valiantly across no man's land.

On the Bank of England's Roll of Honour for those members of staff who served in the armed forces during the First World War, the surname is clearly spelt Palfreymann yet on the Commonwealth War Graves Commission website it is spelt Palfreyman, with only one 'n', as it is on the British Army's medal rolls index cards for the First World War.

Frank Philip Purdie was a clerk at the Bank of England before the outbreak of war. When the war started he joined up and ended up as a major in the 8th Battalion, Essex Regiment. He died of pneumonia on 20 March 1919 whilst home in England and he was buried four days later on Monday 24 March 1919 at 3pm at St Mary's Parish Church in Warwick.

William Horace Stanley Roper was born in London in 1887. He was educated at St Dunstan's College in Catford and then King's College London. At the age of twenty he began working at the Bank of England where he remained for the following nine years, before enlisting and joining the Artists' Rifles Officer Training Corps, in April 1916. By September that year he had become a second lieutenant in the 3rd Battalion, Grenadier Guards. He was twenty-nine years of age when he died of wounds sustained on 11 October 1917. He was buried at the Dozinghem Military Cemetery in the West-Vlaanderen region of Belgium. It was at the nearby 47th Casualty Clearing Station that he died.

According to the De Ruvigny's Roll of Honour, 1914-1919, William's commanding officer wrote the following letter to his parents.

'Your son will be a very great lost to the battalion. He was so very keen at his work, and was very quick at picking it up. He showed tremendous interest in his platoon, and he was always getting up games of football and rounder's for them. He was very good in helping at the battalion concerts and was invariably a most popular item.'

His company commander also wrote.

> 'He had such wonderful spirits, and was a first rate officer in every way. I notice him as we were going up on the evening of the 8th in the pouring rain, how wonderfully he kept up ther spirits of the men.'

There is no entry in the war diaries of the 3rd Battalion, Grenadier Guards for 11 October, the day of William's death, but the entry for 10 October shows them making their way back to Lunaville to rest, recuperate, parade and undergo training. These were their commitments for the rest of October. On 9 October 1917, the battalion were involved in heavy fighting during the Battle of Poelcapelle.

It was during this attack that William received the wounds which resulted in his death two days later. It was a clear day, with a temperature of 53 degrees. The British commanders had originally

The remains of Poelcapelle.

intended for the attack to take place on 9 October but because of excessive, almost continuous rain, between 4 and 9 October, the operation was put back a day.

Wilfred Frederick Sawyer was a private (513882) in the 2nd (London Scottish) Battalion, London Regiment, when he was killed in action on 8 December 1917. He is buried in the Jerusalem War Cemetery. In November 1917, the Egyptian Expeditionary Force were in the process of trying to wrest control of Jerusalem from Turkish Forces. The 60th London Division, which included the London Scottish battalion, were attacking from the west whilst the 53rd Welsh Division were attacking from the south. The fierce fighting lasted until the evening of 8 December 1917, the day on which Private Sawyer was killed. By the following morning the Turkish soldiers had left the city, having used the dark of the night to make good their escape.

Henry French Stephens (Distinguished Service Order, Military Cross) was a major in the 86th Brigade, Royal Field Artillery. He died on 14 October 1918 at the 3rd London General Hospital, Wandsworth, Surrey, where he was having his wounds for gas inhalation treated, just a month before the end of the war. He had initially enlisted in the Army as a rivate (1819) in the City of London Yeomanry (Rough Riders), following his father, Lieutenant-Colonel (Retired) John Naylor Stephens, into the Army. He is buried in the Nunhead Cemetery at the All Saints Church in London.

Herbert Gordon Stuart was twenty-six years of age and a Second Lieutenant in the 3rd Battalion, London Regiment (Royal Fusiliers) when he died of pneumonia on 7 March 1919.

Douglas Clifton Taylor was the youngest of six children born to James and Octavia Taylor. He had three sisters, Ethel, Maud and Florence and two brothers, Thomas Harold and Lawrence Guirard. The family lived at 'Adversane,' Woodcote Avenue, Wallington, Surrey, with five of the family working for the Bank of England, in the City of London. He was twenty-seven years of age and a Lance Corporal (761488) in 'D' Company, 1st/28th Battalion, London Regiment (Artists' Rifles), when he was killed in action on the Western Front on 30 December 1917. He has no known grave and his name is commemorated on the Thiepval Memorial.

George Edward Truby was thirty-four years of age and a second lieutenant in 'D' Company, 2nd Battalion, Lincolnshire Regiment when he was killed in action on 31 July 1917, during fighting in the Battle of Ypres. When he initially enlisted, he did so into the Inns of Court, Officer Training Corps, and quickly became a lance corporal (8889), before being commissioned into the Lincolnshire Regiment on 23 February 1917. He has no known grave and his name is commemorated on the Ypres (Menin Gate) Memorial. Before the war George had been a bank clerk at the Bank of England.

Gerald Vaughan-Jones was a twenty-five year old lieutenant in No.18 Squadron, Royal Flying Corps and the Royal Engineers, when he was killed in action during air combat on 26 February 1917. He is buried at the Guards Cemetery in the village of Lesboeufs, in the Somme region of France.

Before the war Henry Kenneth Weatherhead was a bank clerk, living at the aptly named 'Bank House', Rosemary Road, Clacton-on-Sea, Essex. He enlisted at Westminster, becoming a rifleman (5370) in 'C' Company, 16th (County of London) Battalion London Regiment (Queen's Westminster Rifles). He was killed in action on 10 September 1916 during the bloody fighting at the Battle of the Somme. He is buried in the Combles Communal Cemetery Extension. As the cemetery wasn't actually begun until October 1916, this means that Henry was initially buried elsewhere, most likely at the nearby Leuze Wood Cemetery.

E D Webb was a twenty-five year old sergeant (1061 or 1161) in the 21st Battalion, London Regiment (1st Surrey Rifles), when he was killed in action on 5 May 1915. He is buried at the Le Touret Military Cemetery, Richebourg-L'Avoue, in the Pas de Calais region of France. Sadly for Sergeant Webb he had no known next of kin which meant that there was nobody to send his war time campaign medals to.

Despite a number of its staff going off to fight in the war, the everyday workings of the Bank of England still went ahead as usual, or as usual

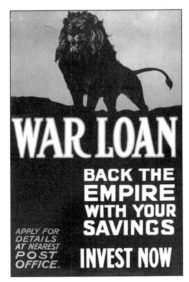

War Loans Posters.

Members of the public purchasing War Loans Bonus's from an outdoors stall, whilst members of the Bank of England staff keep a respectful eye on proceedings.

as it possibly could be in the City of London during the First World War. Even though the nation was embroiled in a war and hundreds of thousands of men were sent off to fight, life still had to carry on as best it could. Businesses needed to be run, children still had to go to school. People still required medical attention for everyday non-war related illnesses and diseases and mothers still had to feed and look after their families, the best way that they could.

The idea behind the war loans scheme was that members of the public would loan the Government much needed money, which for most people would have been their life savings. This helped fund the war effort with the promise of a profitable return on any monies lent, after the war was over. Most of the bonds that were given in return were redeemable from about 1923 onwards. The obvious risks for this scheme, and a sufficient reason which might have proved preventative for some people, was the question of what would have happened to their monies if Britain had lost the war, of if the lender had been killed as a result of the war.

The minimum amount which could be loaned was 5/-, with a very reasonable four and a half per cent interest rate payable when the bond was then later cashed in.

CHAPTER 4

The National Guard

The National Guard, the City of London Volunteers, or even the 'Methusaliers,' as they were known with a mixture of derision and affection, were formed by the Lord Mayor of the City of London, Sir Charles Johnston. The idea of the volunteers unit however came from Mr Henry Bell, the General Manager of Lloyd's Bank and Mr R G H Boulton, but they both knew that to turn their idea into a reality, something which would succeed in the long term, would need the support of a powerful, well known and well respected figure or organisation.

As soon as the pair took their idea to the then Mayor, Sir Charles Johnston, he loved it, and was only too happy to help them turn their dream in to a resounding reality. Recruitment for the new unit began

The Cap badge of the National Guard.

at number 99 Gresham Street, and the man behind the desk dealing with all of the enquiries was Oswald Bell, who was the National Guard's Secretary. The numbers wanting to join up were too much for one man to deal with so reinforcements were called upon in the shape of volunteers. But these were not just any old volunteers, these were people who had reached the very top of military leadership. There was Captain Burder-Dunning and Captain I Watt; Brigadier-General Abbott and last but not least, Colonel R K Ridgeway, VC, CB. who had been awarded the Victoria Cross in 1879 during the 2nd Naga Hill Expedition.

The conditions of being allowed to join the National Guard in the Great War, were not stringent, Members had to be 40 years of age or older and be British born citizens; neither neutral aliens nor naturalised citizens were to be accepted. Members had to pay a yearly subscription and provide their own firearm and uniform.

The beginning of the National Guard is accepted as being 26 December 1914, when the Lord Mayor called a meeting at the Guildhall in the City of London. It was by invitation only. The Lord Mayor opened proceedings and then handed over to Colonel Cobbett who explained what would be expected of those who joined the National Guard.

Active drill for the inaugural 1500 members commenced on 1 January 1915 and took place at the Headquarters of the 7th Battalion, London Regiment, in Sun Street. The Guildhall itself was used as was the Headquarters of the London Rifle Brigade in Bunhill Row, whilst others had to drill outdoors at the City of London School playground, Clifford's Inn and Temple Gardens.

Although universally referred to as The National Guard, the unit's official affiliated title with the Central Volunteer Association was, 'The City of London National Guard Volunteers.'

A decision had to be taken in relation to what uniform members should wear. The original intention had been for a dark blue jacket and trousers or breeches, but this was eventually changed to what had become the accepted and recognised uniform of the Volunteer Training Corps, of grey/green tunic and trousers, with the same style of peak cap worn by the Regular Army and Territorial Forces. There was a noticeable difference in the style of jacket that an officer would wear as opposed to what a man from the other ranks would wear.

Lord Mayor, Sir Thomas Vansittart Bowater & Lord Kitchener inspect members of the National Guard at the Guildhall, August 1914.

Initially members were provided with Springfield rifles in the form of a donation from Francis Bannerman, from New York, who also happened to be a patriotic Scotsman. This allowed for the men to practice with and get used to handling firearms at the earliest opportunity, rather than have to wait until the British authorities were able to provide them with the more up to date and modern, Lee Enfield rifles, which were being used by British soldiers on the Western Front and in other theatres of war.

The Corps' first route march took place on 23 January 1915 when they marched from the Mansion House to Hyde Park. They were joined

PRIVATE.
Original Pattern.)

OFFICER.
(The Rank Mark is that of a
Company Commander.)

PRIVATE.
(Permissible Alternative Style.)

UNIFORMS.

Drawings of National Guard uniforms (Central Volunteer Association)

on their journey by the Band of the Duke of Connaught's Hussars, the Lord Mayor of the City of London, Colonel Ridgeway, VC, CB, and Sir John Leigh Wood, CB, CMG.

March 1915 was an extremely memorable month for the Corps. Having parading in uniform for the first time in Hyde Park on 6 March, an event which was witnessed by Queen Alexandra and Princess Victoria, they followed that up on 23 March when they were inspected by the king himself in the grounds of Buckingham Palace. There were a total of 47 officers and 2046 men of other ranks. The men set off from Mansion House and the Guildhall and their route took them along the Embankment and the River Thames before continuing along Horse Guards Avenue and then on to Buckingham Palace. It was a grand event with the Lord Mayor also present, taking his place to the right of the king on the balcony overlooking the Palace gardens, along with other senior dignitaries of the Home Guard.

April did not provide them with any respite. For six days in early

April 1915, 1,400 members of the National Guard went to Brighton to take part in manoeuvres over the Easter Bank Holiday weekend, not arriving back in London until late on the Tuesday evening.

At the end of his year in office as the Lord Mayor of the City of London, Sir Charles Johnston said the following,

> 'If you ask me of what I am most proud of having accomplished during my term, I should unhesitatingly reply, the establishment of that splendid body of men, the National Guard of the City of London. I rejoice to have taken the leading part in its inception and incorporation.'

So enamoured with the National Guard was Sir Charles, that after his year in office he remained as the Hon. Regimental Commandant of the Corps. When the National Guard later became part of the City of London Volunteer Regiment, Sir Charles was not to be deterred, and became the Colonel of the 5th Battalion. At the signing of the Armistice and with the fighting finally over, the National Guard as part of the City of London Volunteer Regiment was disbanded and became part of London's history. But still Sir Charles could not abandon his commitment to what he had been largely responsible for bringing in to being, so he became the President of the 5th Battalion's Old Comrades Association.

Their purpose in essence was to guard and protect the City of London. Those who volunteered to serve in the National Guard were predominantly older men, some of whom were old soldiers who had served in previous wars and conflicts but were now too old or no longer physically fit enough to serve in the armed forces. Some were those who had been rejected from enlisting in the Army on medical grounds, but all of them still wanted to do their bit for the war effort. They numbered some 2,000 in total, an extremely formidable volunteer force by any standard, especially in a time of war. For a lot of these men, who were still in full time employment, to be willing to commit their evenings and Sundays to the defence of the City of London, showed remarkable dedication. Despite all of this, in some quarters they were still seen as nothing more than knackered old men who were best off in front of the fire warming their weary feet.

They protected railway stations, prominent buildings, they guarded prisoners of war, all tasks which no longer had to be carried out by soldiers, so increasing the number of young, able-bodied men who were available to go off and fight. It must have been difficult, even embarrassing for a young man who hadn't offered himself up for enlistment, seeing an old man in uniform, maybe even with a beard, doing his bit.

The men of the National Guard did what they did voluntarily and willingly, with no pay and no desire for applause or thanks for their efforts. Like an old masterpiece, their full value would not be truly appreciated until many years later, when all that was left of what they once did and stood for was no more than a distant memory or a fading image of an old black and white photograph. For many who were members of the National Guard it filled a void in their life, it gave them a sense of purpose, a spirit of adventure and excitement which they had previously known and enjoyed, but which they had long ago left behind them. For some, being a member of the National Guard did just as much for them as they did for it. At a time of their lives when many were weighed down with the burdens and responsibilities of adult life, doing their bit in the evenings and at the weekends gave many of them a new lease of life, a new direction and impetus, their feeling of self worth and purpose having once more returned.

On 1 March 1915 Hansard records that Sir John Rees, the Member of Parliament for Nottingham East, raised the question of uniforms for men of the National Guard. It started a lively discussion, a debate which lasted for some forty-one minutes. Sir John was trying to establish whether the War Office approved of the volunteers, who were the brainchild of the Lord Mayor, Colonel Sir Charles Johnston, and if they did, would they be happy for them to wear a military style uniform? The question, intentionally or otherwise, highlighted in part how 'red tape' put in place by Government made a perfectly straight forward process appear extremely complicated, as well as also ever so slightly ridiculous. Part of the main issue was whether or not the Central Association of Volunteer Training Corps, who approved all uniforms worn by Volunteer Corps, actually had the backing from the War Office to make such decisions.

The situation became even more ridiculous when it was pointed out by Sir John that although the rules of the Volunteer Training Corps advised that the wearing of a Brassard was compulsory with a uniform, a Brassard was in fact a subsitute that was normally worn with civillian clothes to advise others that the person wearing it was acting in an official capacity.

Sir William Bull, the Member of Parliament for Hammersmith, joined the discussion, asking for clarification on a particular point made in a lettter that had been written by Sir Reginald Brade to Lord Desborough on 19 November 1914. His point highlighted the issue surrounding Volunteer Training Corps and the Government's view in relation to them. At the time such corps had not been officially sanctioned by the War Office, the issue was who controlled them and who made the rules by which they operated. Sir William quoted from the letter.

'It will be open to an Army recruiting officer to visit the Corps at any time, and recruit any members found eligible for service with the Regular Army whose presence in the Corps is not accounted for by some good and sufficient reason.'

Even though he understood the need for the Government to have some control over Volunteer Corps, his point was that the above paragraph was in fact a back-handed form of conscription; so to make the matter easier why not actually bring it in so that there would no longer be any ambiguities, and at least anybody who believed they had a genuine reason not to go off to war had a means and a structure in place by which they could appeal the decision to make them enlist.

Sir William's wish would be realised the following year when conscription was brought in by the Government. He saw such a move as a positive step to help quell the mis-belief that being in the Volunteer Corps would prevent anyone called upon to serve their country from having to do so. He pointed out that the majority of Volunteer Corps went to great lengths to advertise that they did not want men who were fit enough and young enough to serve in the Regular Army.

Sir John's question was answered by Mr Tennant, who at the time was the Under-Secretary of State for War. He advised that any such authorisation in relation to the wearing of a uniform by a Volunteer Corps did not come from the War Office but from the Central Association of Volunteer Corps, as long as they adhered to the rules which governed such matters. He also commented in relation to

Brassards; he agreed with Sir John's stance on the matter, but pointed out that the Government could not be held responsible for decisions made by the Central Association of Volunteer Corps, of which Lord Desborough was the President. He also commented on the issue of conscription, in which he suggesting by his words that it was not a path that the Government was looking to go down. 'We can only use the power of persuasion,' he said, before continuing, 'I should like to relieve the House of any apprehension they may have on that subject by informing them that all the powers of persuasion are being used. I would add how greatly we appreciated the great self sacrifice of the men who are joining these Corps.'

Mr Tennant's comments showed just how quickly matters could change in a time of war. On the assuption that what he said concerning conscription was a truthful and honest response on behalf of the Government, it also showed just how badly the war was going for Britain and her allies in relation to the issue of having sufficient men available to effectively continue the fight against Germany and her allies. It also showed just how poor the overall standard and quality of her senior officers were, in a tactical sense, with the continuing high losses of so many men in the field. It was almost as if arrogance prevailed towards the common soldier. The Battle of the Somme was a prime example; it took the loss of 450,000 British soldiers, before General Haig called a halt to the slaughter, after having gained only five miles of territory over a four month period.

There were undoubtedly some cases where men from the National Guard did voluntarily go on to enlist in the Regular Army during the First World War. The National Guard had many different sections and was not just a group of well meaning elderly men marching up and down everytime there was a ceremony that required men in uniform to be present. Besides consisting of a 4th, 5th, and 6th Battalions, there was a Machine Gun section; musketry staff; medical staff; an ambulance section; a mechanical transport section; an engineers unit and one for Pioneers and Guides; signalling scouts; a cyclists' section and a band.

In May 1915 468 members of the National Guard went to a location 'somewhere in Essex' to dig trenches which formed part of the North London Defence System. One such location where trenches were being dug for that very reason was Billericay, which is a rural town situated between Basildon and Chelmsford. The trenches there were also used by soldiers training to go off to war. It was the same situation in different locations just north of Brentwood. Whilst at their Essex camp, discipline was strict, including being up sharp at 6 am to be ready for parade and drill an hour later. Breakfast was at 7.45 am and the parade in readiness to go off trench digging for the day was at 10.15 am. At the end of the day men not only had to be in bed by 10 pm, but lights had to be out and no talking was allowed. A very strict regime for a group of volunteers.

Although it was work that had to be done, the fact it was done by a group of volunteers, most of whom were in their 50s and 60s, and whose day to day work was mainly office based and certainly not a role which included arduous labour, made it an even more remarkable achievement.

Wednesday 9 June 1915 saw some 1500 officers and men of the National Guard attend a Church Parade at St Paul's Cathedral in the City of London, where the sermon was given by the Lord Bishop of London. He spoke of how Britain was fighting a just and proper war

The National Guard at a City Fete 16 June 1915.

The National Guard at St Paul's Cathedral Wednesday 9 June 1915.

in good conscience before God, which was the reason why, he suggested, that the nation was bearing its situation with strength and happiness.

Members of the National Guard as well as their families, took every opportunity not only to advertise the sterling work that they did, but also to try and encourage other such well-meaning individuals, who for whatever reason were unable to enlist in the regular Army or Territorial Force, to join them.

A National Guard Friend helping out two returning soldiers.

Members of the National Guard would act as a 'friend' and 'mentor' for battle weary soldiers returning from 'the front' on leave, at one of the capital's numerous railway stations. The idea was to direct the soldiers as to the best and quickest way for them to get home to their loved ones, so that they didn't waste any of their very precious time spent away from the stresses of the war.

Members of the National Guard would help protect most of the main line railway stations throughout the capital, as they did in the above photograph at Kings Cross. Yet another case of helping out wherever they were needed. There are forty-five men in the

National Guard members at Kings Cross Railway Station.

photograph, voluntarily doing a job that would have otherwise required the same amount of soldiers to do, men who were urgently required to fight the war. The other London main railway stations which were covered by men from the National Guard were Euston, Waterloo, Kings Cross and Victoria.

September 1915 was an interesting and an exciting time for members of the National Guard. Every member of the corps received a notice informing them that a group of not less than 500 of them would be accepted to work in France digging trenches for a period of one month. Some saw it as an opportunity to go and be able to say that they really had done their bit for the war effort, others weren't interested as they had purely signed up for home defence. There were others who wanted to go but who couldn't because of health, business or domestic reasons and some were annoyed that they were being asked to go but only to dig trenches and not to fight. Despite all of these variables, 400 men had already indicated a strong desire to go, within a matter of days of having received their notices.

Excitement and anticipation were at fever pitch as preparations for the men's departure drew nearer. The Lord Mayor had arranged for those men who were going, to be inspected by him at the Guildhall on Friday 8 October 1915, before their departure. Sadly for the men, and totally unexpectedly, a message was received from the War Office, that because of the conditions that existed in France, Sir John French did not think it was suitable for the members of the National Guard to be sent overseas at that time. This seemed to be somewhat of a strange decision when compared to, say, conscientious objectors, many of whom had been forced to join units such as the Non Combatants Corps or the Royal Army Medical Corps, mainly to act as stretcher bearers or Ambulance drivers, and who quite often found themselves being sent to the Western Front in France or Belgium. Nurses were sent to every theatre of war that British and Allied forces were fighting in, and although there were those in the military who believed that being at the front and dealing with badly wounded soldiers, was no place for a woman, they still went. Some were awarded gallantry medals for their bravery and some were killed doing their duty of caring for wounded and sick soldiers.

Sir Charles 'Cheers' Wakefield in National Guard uniform.

The Lord Mayor's show took place on 9 November 1915 with the inauguration of Colonel Sir Charles Wakefield as the new Lord Mayor.

A detachment of some 200 members of the National Guard took part in that year's show. Most of the men were drawn from those who had previously volunteered to serve overseas. There were numerous other detachments from different branches of the military taking part and the detachment from the National Guard more than held their own in appearance and marching. It wasn't a particularly nice day for any kind of march, especially one as important as the one for the Lord Mayor's show. It was a cold overcast day, with rain being the main element.

In part, the National Guard lost its singular identity in the early part of 1916, when it became part of the City of London Volunteer Regiment, in particular the 4th, 5th, and 6th Battalions, officially becoming a group. The National Guard's Regimental Commandant, Colonel Corbett, became a Group Commandant.

The Oath that Corps members now had to swear was as follows.

'I do sincerely promise and swear that I will be faithful and bear true allegiance to his Majesty King George the Fifth, and that I will faithfully serve his majesty in Great Britain for the defence

The National Guard march past Mansion House April 1916.

of the same against all his enemies and opposers what so ever, according to the conditions of my service.'

Whilst still the Lord Mayor, Sir Charles 'Cheers' Wakefield, was appointed as a lieutenant-colonel in the City of London Regiment and the County Commandant. His appointment was announced in the 'London Gazette' on 1 September 1916. He also later became the honorary colonel of the 2nd City of London Regiment (The Royal Fusiliers). His support of the National Guard and the armed forces in general during the war, could not have been made any more obvious or personal. He was a true and loyal supporter of them in every sense of the word.

Now that the National Guard was part of the City of London Volunteer Regiment, their numbers started to decrease, but not for any one particular reason. The reduction in numbers was actually a good thing, because it meant getting rid of some dead wood, which would gradually and naturally occur in most similar organisations.

With the outbreak of war came a national fervour, a desire to do one's bit, an enthusiasm to be part of something that they could tell their grandchildren about. When the war was over, nobody wanted to be thought of as a shirker or a coward. As time went on that initial flush of enthusiasm had waned somewhat. There was no imminent end in sight.

For lots of the men who were now well in to their fifties, the training was becoming harder and harder; for some of them it was failing health that had caused them to quit. Others could no longer sustain their businesses and work side by side with their commitment to the National Guard.

The determining factor for a lot of the men was having to sign an attestation when the National Guard became incorporated into the City of London Volunteer Regiment, because now they were part of his Majesty's Armed Forces and as such had to adhere to military rules and discipline. Signing this document meant that there was a real chance of being called up if Germany invaded Great Britain, when London would have been one of the obvious early targets. Having

Memorial to Lord Wakefield, Trinity Square, London.

become part of the City of the London Volunteer Regiment, there was now no longer the need or requirement to wear their hated red brassard, which had most definitely not been worn as a badge of honour, but more a mark of ridicule.

It was on the 17 June 1916 that some 10,000 Volunteers from all across London were reviewed at Horse Guards Parade before marching to Hyde Park. Those from the National Guard numbered 1,587 officers and men. It was a truly amazing occasion. The weather was most agreeable, warm without being too hot, with clear blue skies and the gentlest of breezes.

To show just how well thought of and how much the Government needed its Volunteer units, the very cream of the crop, senior officers as well as other dignitaries, were all in attendance. In no particular order they were: the Lord Mayor; the Duke of Rutland; Lord Desborough; Viscount Churchill; Earl Brownlow; Major-General Sir Desmond O'Callaghan; Colonel Sir Douglas Dawson; Colonel Sir

George Holford; Sir William Collins; Mr Percy A Harris, who was the Honorary Secretary of the Central Associations of the Volunteer Training Corps; Major-General Sir Francis Lloyd, who was the general officer commanding of the London District; and General Sir O'Moore Creagh, VC. The man they were all waiting for was Lord French, who carried out the inspection on horseback, which took him just twenty minutes before he gathered the commanding officers of the various regiments who were present. He began by offering the king's apologies for not being able to attend the occasion in person and carry out the review himself and how he appreciated their continuing devoted loyalty and energy. Lord French went on to address them with a continuous list of platitudes concerning their achievements, their effectiveness and for their worthiness as a respected part of the British Army.

Men of the National Guard proudly marching past the Lord Mayor of the City of London, Sir William Henry Dunn, in November 1916, outside the Mansion House, soon after he took office.

Four members of the National Guard being inspected by one of their officers as they stand guard at the Thames Tunnel entrance in 1916.

Sir William had an affinity with volunteers, having been an officer in the Army's Territorial Force in his younger days. The crowds of well-wishers showed just how an auspicious an occasion such events were, especially with the added slice of national fervour during war time.

January 1917 saw the National Guard, as well as other volunteer units, finally receive official recognition they had been waiting and hoping for, since the war had begun, when His Royal Highness, The Duke of Connaught, became their Commander-in-Chief. His appointment was at about the same time that Field-Marshal Viscount French returned from the Western Front to take command of the Home Forces. He was suitably impressed by the professionalism displayed by the volunteer units, and took no time in letting them know the importance and worth which he placed on their continuous efforts. Soon after his return to England, Field Marshal French, carried out an inspection of Volunteer Forces, at Hyde Park in London, and passed on the following message.

'His Majesty the King values and appreciates his Volunteer Force as much as any other, and the War Office and the Government want their services.'

Knowing that they were held in such high esteem by the authorities and their king, meant a great deal to all of the men of the volunteer forces. It had taken nearly three years to receive such recognition for their continued contributions, making everything they had done worthwhile. No longer were they made to feel like the 'poor relations'. They could be rightly proud of what they had achieved and what they stood for, especially as they had been doing their bit for the war effort since hostilities had begun.

Another way in which the National Guard gained new recruits was via Military Service Tribunals. If a man was successful in his appeal against having to go off to war and fight, either temporarily or permanently, he could quite often find himself having to serve with the National Guard. Very rarely was a man who was successful in his appeal at such a tribunal let off entirely without having to carry out some kind of official war service.

The following is a poem about the National Guard by one of its members, R.C.Russell.

THE NATIONAL GUARD
We had long joy of slumberous days,
basked in the sunshine of our ease.
Until the dawn of War's red rays,
flashed on our city, land and seas.
Then once again the clear call rang,
through storied tower and ward and shine.
'To arms!' the old familiar clang,
'Leave the feasting and the wine,'
It was the call our London knew,
dim years ago when in our pride,
she seaward hurried a corsair crew.
Past Thanet, from the grey Thames tide,
down the fierce centuries that viewed.
The building of our hearts desire,
each signal, for the fray and feud,

re-lit the dauntless civic fire.
And when the mother of us all
waged war beneath the southern stars,
her London heard the bugles call,
her train bands shared the brunt and scars.
Domestic weather of today
though not upon the shell-torn field,
we stand as brothers in the fray.
and help to bear the island shield.

The National Guard were finally disbanded in 1920 after nearly six years of hard work and endeavours for the City of London, in protecting and assisting those who lived, worked and travelled through it.

CHAPTER 5

London Territorials, London Regiments

Officers of 3rd/6th Battalion City of London Rifles

The above photograph appeared in the Illustrated War News dated 22 September 1915 and shows a group of officers of the 3rd/6th Battalion, City of London Rifles, a Territorial Unit, outside their headquarters which was at number 57 Farringdon Road, London. The Battalion originally arrived in France in March 1915 and was involved in its first action at the Battle of Loos, in September of that year. It remained in France until the end of the war.

The names of the twenty-three men in the photograph, from left to right and starting with the back row are:

Lieutenant H R Woodcock

Lieutenant H T Ordish

Lieutenant A B Westcombe

Lieutenant H R Perry

Lieutenant G W Hammond

Lieutenant J J Ball

Lieutenant J N Terry

Lieutenant F H Butler

Lieutenant J G Gregory

Lieutenant V Simmonds

The men in the middle row, once again, going from left to right are;

2nd Lieutenant H C Glayzer

Lieutenant G Cotton

Lieutenant E D Stokes

Lieutenant E A Upcott

Lieutenant S Craven

2nd Lieutenant R J Heath
  Brown

And the men seated in the front row are;

Captain T E Painton Jones

Adjutant G Valentine

Captain E Clay

Lieutenant & Quarter Master
  F G Lovett

Captain M J Macdonald

Major E Stokes

Lieutenant T W Wardhaugh

By the end of the war six of the young men in the photograph would sadly be dead, having paid the ultimate price in serving their king and country in their hour of need. Captain G Valentine, 6th Battalion London Regiment (City of London Rifles) was killed in action 15 September 1916 during the Battle of Flers-Courcelette, which is remembered for the fact that it was where British forces used tanks for the first time in the war. The village of Flers was captured from the Germans by Commonwealth forces on the same day that Captain Valentine was killed. The first burials did not take place there until 19 September, making Valentine one of the first to be buried at what became known as Bull's Road Cemetery in Flers, which is situated in the Somme region of France.

Henry Thomas Ordish was a Captain in 'B' Company, 6th Battalion, London Regiment (City of London). He died of his wounds on 25 March 1918 aged thirty-seven and was a holder of the Military Cross. He is buried at the Cambrai East Military Cemetery, in the Nord region of France. He was thirty-seven years of age. There is some suggestion that at the time of his death he was being held by the Germans as a prisoner of war. Henry had two younger brothers, the middle one, who was twelve years his junior, was 2nd Lieutenant Bernard William Arthur Ordish. He was a member of 22 Squadron Royal Flying Corps, and acting as an observer on 9 November 1916, when he was shot down and captured. He was repatriated to England on 7 September 1918. He had originally been a private (1664) in the 28th Battalion, London Regiment. His younger brother, Firman John Ordish, served as a captain in the Essex Regiment during the First World War and survived, arriving in France on 6 May 1918 when he was twenty-three years of age.

John Norman Terry was a captain in the 6th Battalion, London Regiment. He died from wounds inflicted by an exploding German grenade on 20 September 1916 whilst he was bravely attacking an enemy machine gun position near Flers, during the bloody fighting at the battle of the Somme. He inspired his men by carrying out an act of bravery which he must have known would result in his own death. Before the war he had been studying medicine at St Thomas's Hospital in London, where he was a member of the Officer Training Corp, before transferring to the Artists' Rifles at the outbreak of the war. The Artists' Rifles were based at Gidea Hall in Romford. He initially became a private (3125) in the 28th Battalion, London Regiment, before being commissioned as a 2nd lieutenant in the 6th Battalion of the same regiment where he was promoted to the rank of captain. He is buried at the Heilly Station Cemetery just outside the village of Mericourt-L'Abbe, which is situated in the Somme region of France. In his will he left his elder brother, Leonard Hankinson Terry, who was a captain in the Royal Army Medical Corp, the sum of £2098. Leonard survived the war.

Frederick Harold Butler was a 2nd lieutenant in 6th Battalion, London Regiment (City of London Rifles) when he was killed in action on 1 January 1916. He has no known grave and his name is commemorated on the Loos War Memorial which is located in the Pas de Calais region of France.

Loos Memorial and Cemetery (Commonwealth War Graves Commission)

Leslie Roy Perry was a twenty year old 2nd lieutenant in the 6th Battalion, London Regiment (City of London Rifles) when he was killed in action on 15 September 1916. He has no known grave and his name is commemorated on the Thiepval War Memorial which can be found in the Somme region of France. Leslie had two brothers, Percy Victor Perry and Sydney James Perry. Percy had already emigrated to Canada before the start of the war where he enlisted in the 143rd Overseas Battalion, Canadian Expeditionary Force, on 14 February 1916. He survived the war. Official records show that there was a Sidney James Perry who had initially served as a private 3167 in the 9th Battalion, London Regiment before being commissioned and going on to reach the rank of lieutenant in the 6th Battalion, London Regiment.

John George Gregory was a 2nd lieutenant in the 6th Battalion, London Regiment (City of London Rifles) when he died of his wounds on 8 January 1916, just three months after the group photograph with his fellow officers was taken. He is buried at the Noeux-Les-Mines communal cemetery in the Pas-de-Calais region of France. Before the war he had worked as a clerk at a local gas works.

The Band of the 6th Battalion, London Regiment.

The war changed the lives of these men in so many different ways. Most had never even contemplated joining any branch of the armed forces, let alone going off to fight in a bloody war, but when the call to arms came, most simply quit their jobs and joined up without hesitation.

(56). Men of the 6th Battalion, London Regiment.

Unlike the officers in the main photograph at the beginning of the chapter, whose names have been recorded, the men from the Other Ranks, either the ones in the band or those sitting round the table whilst enjoying a meal and each other's company, have not, so it has not been possible to determine who amongst them survived the war and who perished in it. A quarter of the officers in the photograph did not survive the war so sadly there is every possibility that a similar percentage of men, possibly even more, from the Other Ranks did not either.

Officers of the 6th Battalion, London Regiment.

During the First World War there were numerous regiments which had connections with the capital. The London Regiment, which was first formed in 1908, managed to raise a mind boggling ninety different battalions, which in part was due to the city's wide and varied diversity. Eighty-two of these battalions saw action during the war. Fourteen of them saw action in Palestine, six of them served during the Gallipoli campaign, twelve went to Salonika and forty-nine of them were on the Western Front in France and Flanders. From these battalions a total of 9,582 officers and men would lose their lives as a result of the part that they played in the war. There were Regular Army battalions as well as Territorial units. So great was the desire by lots of young men to want to join up and do their bit, that some units had to raise two or three battalions to cater for those who wished to enlist. So often was this the case that they were more like Pals Regiments.

The 1st (City of London) Battalion (Royal Fusiliers), The London Regiment, was a Territorial unit, which at the outbreak of the war was part of the 1st London Brigade which in turn was part of the 1st London Division. They were mobilized immediately war broke out and were initially tasked with guarding the London to Newhaven railway line from any attempts at sabotage.

The following photograph of officers and men of the 1st Battalion, must have been taken not only after the war but sometime in to the early 1920's, as most of the men are wearing groups of medals, one would assume awarded to them for their service during the First World War. Most of the campaign medals from the war were not actually issued until 1921/1922.

A month into the war the battalion was sent to Malta, leaving Southampton on 4 September 1914 and arriving in Valetta ten days later. It can only be imagined as to how the men felt on that journey. Even though the seas might have appeared calm on the surface, the

1st (City of London) Battalion London Regiment (Royal Fusiliers)

ever present fear of a German submarine prowling the depths underneath them, could not have been far from their thoughts, or a comfortable feeling either. It certainly would not have been a relaxing cruise. The task of the battalion was to replace units of the Regular Army who were stationed in Malta so that they in turn could be released and sent to France as part of the British Expeditionary Force. As it was, the Royal Fusiliers only remained in Malta for five months, leaving there on 11 February 1915 and arriving back in England at Avonmouth ten days later. They were back home for less than a month before they arrived at Le Havre on 11 March where they were literarily thrown straight in to the thick of things at the battle of Neuve Chapelle, which took place between 10 and 13 March. They saw action again on 9 May at the battle of Aubers and were also involved in the action against defending German forces at Bois Grenier on 25 September..

The following year was to see no respite for them in the fighting as they were involved in the attack at Gommecourt which was a diversionary action on the very first day of the battle of the Somme on 1 July 1916. Later in the year, but also as part of the main battle of the Somme, they also saw action at Ginchy on 9 September, Flers-Courcelette between 15 and 22 September, Morval, between 25 and 28 September and the Transloy Ridges, between 1 and 18 October.

In 1917 they saw further action at Arras between 9 April and 16 May, when Commonwealth and South African troops attacked German defensive positions there. Although by the end of the battle the Allied forces had made significant advances they had not gained an overall decisive victory, but had incurred 158,000 casualties. Three months later they once again saw action at Langemarck, between 16 and 18 August which took place during the Third Battle of Ypres.

During what would turn out to be the final year of the war the battalion saw more action at the second Battle of Arras, 26 August to 3 September 1918; the battles of the Hindenburg Line which went on for a month between 12 September to 12 October; and the final advance into Picardy which started on 17 October and finished with the signing of the Armistice and the end of the war on 11 November.

There were three battalions of the Post Office Rifles, the 8th, 2/8th, and the 3/8th Battalions, City of London Regiment and although all Territorial units, they were all in France by March 1915.

The Commonwealth War Graves Commission records a total of

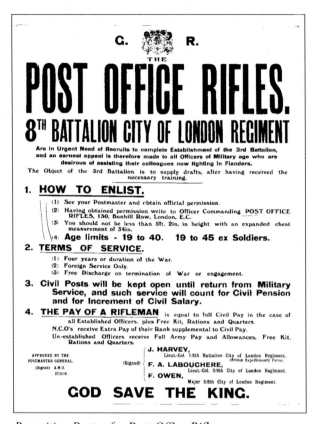

Recruiting Poster for Post Office Rifles.

1,542 men from the Post Office Rifles as having been killed during the First World War. Of these, two were Mentioned in Despatches, twenty-six were awarded the Military Medal, seven were awarded the Military Cross, three were awarded the Distinguished Conduct Medal. One officer, Major Home Peel, was awarded the Distinguished Service Order having already been awarded the Military Cross whilst Captain Reginald Horace Arthur Newsome was Mentioned in Despatches twice, and was also awarded a Military Cross for his acts of gallantry. By the end of the war the officers and men of the Post Office Rifles had been awarded a total of 145 medals for gallantry including one Victoria Cross to Sergeant Alfred Knight.

Officers of 3rd/2nd Battalion, London Regiment (Royal Fusiliers) 1915.

The 3rd/2nd Battalion, London Regiment (Royal Fusiliers) were one of the seventy-six battalions that were raised during the First World War who wore the Fusiliers cap badge.

Of the eighteen men in the above photograph only two would not survive the war. Second Lieutenant Harry R Barton was twenty-four years of age when he was killed in action on 22 March 1918. He has no known grave and his name is commemorated on the Pozieres War Memorial which is situated in the Somme Region of France.

Second Lieutenant William Philip Stevens was killed on 31 August 1918 and at the time of his death he was attached to the 1st/18th Battalion, London Regiment (London Irish Rifles). His name is commemorated on the Vis-en-Artois War Memorial which is situated in the Pas de Calais region of France.

Pozieres Memorial (Commonwealth War Graves Commission)

Statue of London Regiments of the First World War

The statue, which sits immediately opposite the Bank of England, commemorates the names of the London based Regiments that took part in the First World War. The main unit was the London Regiment which was originally raised in 1908 with twenty-six battalions, but which during the war, rose to ninety-two, making it the biggest regiment in the British Army, so big in fact that its numbers were twice the size of today's entire British Army The regiments and battalions which are listed on the statue, besides being regiments from the capital, also included men who either worked or lived in the City of London. Amongst others are:

Royal Fusiliers (City of London) Regiment
The Honourable Artillery Company
Post Office Rifles
Queen Victoria Rifles
Hackney Rifles
Finsbury Rifles
The Rangers
Kensington Battalion
London Scottish
Prince of Wales Own Civil Service Rifles
Queens Westminster Rifles
Poplar & Stepney Rifles
London Irish Rifles
St Pancras Battalion
Blackheath & Woolwich Battalion
Surrey Rifles
The Queens Battalion
 Cyclist Battalion
Artists Rifles
(City of London) Battalion (Rifle Brigade)
(City of London) Battalion (King's Royal Rifle Corps)
Royal Army Service Corps (London Units)
Royal Army Medical Corps (London Units)
Royal Army Veterinary Corps (London Units)
Territorial Force Nursing Service (London Division)
Voluntary Aid Detachments

There were three Yeomanry battalions:
    City of London (Rough Riders)
    Westminster Dragoons
    County of London (Sharp Shooters).

There were four Engineering battalions.
    1st Battalion, London Divisional Royal Engineers
    2nd Battalion, London Divisional Royal Engineers (London
       Electrical Engineers)
    London Army Troops Royal Engineers

There were ten Artillery units made up from the Field and Garrison Artillery. Of these battalions, forty-nine saw action in either France or Belgium. Fourteen battalions saw action in Palestine, twelve on the Salonika Front, another six battalions in the Gallipoli campaign, and one battalion was in Afghanistan. The officers and men who formed these regiments were drawn from all parts of London and came from different social classes. Some of the regiments had royal connections, as well as others which had an individual element to them such as the Post Office and Artists battalions.

During the First World War the Victoria Cross was awarded on 628 occasions and no doubt there could and should have been many more similar awards for numerous other acts of bravery that were either not witnessed by anyone else or everybody involved in the incident was killed. In 1914 there were 46 Victoria Crosses awarded. In 1915 that figure increased to 117. In 1916 there were 84 awarded. The following year saw that figure more than double to 174 and in the eleven months of 1918, the Victoria Cross was awarded on an incredible 207 occasions, the last one awarded for an act of bravery on 6 November 1918. The first two VCs of the war were awarded to two members of the 4th Battalion, Royal Fusiliers, (City of London Regiment). Lieutenant Maurice Dease and Private Sidney Frank Godley. By the time the war had started Godley had already been in the army for nearly five years. His 'moment' of glory came about on 23 August 1914 during the Battle of Mons. Along with his comrades he was in a defensive position set up on the Mons side of the Mons-Conde Canal, immediately adjacent to the Nimy Railway Bridge. The British defenders were eventually forced to retreat by a much larger number of advancing troops from the German First Army, and the sudden and unannounced retreat of the French Fifth Army, who were on the British right flank. The Germans sustained heavy casualties in their attempts at dislodging their dogged British foe. British casualties were more than 1,500 but the remaining forces managed to withdraw, in no large part thanks to the efforts of Private Godley and Lieutenant Dease. Maurice Dease took charge of one of the battalion's Vickers machine guns after other members of his unit who had been firing it had either been killed or wounded. He was wounded five times before he would allow himself to be removed and taken to a nearby aid station, where he died soon after.

Private Sidney Frank Godley, VC.

Godley carried on firing the machine gun for more than two hours until he ran out of ammunition, to enable his comrades to make good their escape, knowing that he was facing almost certain death. Despite sustaining a shrapnel wound to his back and a gunshot wound to his head, he managed to dismantle his machine gun, discarding pieces of it in to the river, therefore preventing it from falling in to the hands of the Germans. Godley was taken prisoner and spent the rest of the war at a camp at Dallgow-Doberitz, which is where he was informed of his award. He was presented with his medal on 15 February 1919 by George V, during a ceremony at Buckingham Palace.

Geoffrey Woolley holds the distinction of being the first officer from the Territorial Army to be awarded the Victoria Cross. The Allies captured the location known as Hill 60 on 17 April 1915, which was to the south-east of the Belgian town of Ypres. This was immediately met with a dogged attempt by German forces to retake the Hill. Woolley and his company were tasked on 20 April 1915 with supplying

2nd Lieutenant Geoffrey Harold Woolley (VC, OBE, MC) of the 9th (County of London) Battalion, London Regiment (Queen Victoria's Rifles).

ammunition to the Allied units defending the Hill. Despite their actions matters quickly became critical when the defending units lost all of the officers and a lot of their men. Despite numerous orders to withdraw Woolley and his company stayed on the Hill throughout the night, repelling repeated German attacks. By the time they were relieved the following morning, the company, which had started out with 150 men, had only 14 left alive. Woolley survived the war but stayed in the army until he resigned his commission in 1923 to become the parish priest in Monk Sherbourne in Hampshire.

Lance Sergeant Douglas Walter Belcher of the 1st/5th (City of London) Battalion, London Regiment (The London Rifle Brigade) was awarded the Victoria Cross for his actions on 13 May 1915. At Julien Road in Belgium, during a continuous German artillery bombardment of his position, and after the troops around him had been withdrawn, he stayed behind, firing on the enemy who were only a short distance away. In doing so he prevented them from conducting an attack on a weakened section of the Allied defences. Douglas survived the war and went on to serve in the Second World War.

Lance-Sergeant Douglas Walter Belcher VC.

Lance Corporal (3026) Leonard James Keyworth VC, of the 1st/24th Battalion. The *London Gazette* of 2 July 1915 gave the following account of his act of bravery:

'His Majesty the King has been graciously pleased to approve of the award of the Victoria Cross to No. 3026 Lance Corporal Leonard James Keyworth, 24th (County of London) Battalion, The London Regiment (The Queen's) Territorial Force. For most conspicuous bravery at Givenchy on the night of 25/26 May 1915. After the assault on the German position by the 24th Battalion, London Regiment, efforts were made by that Unit to follow up their success by a bomb attack, during the progress of which 58 men out of a total of 75 became casualties. During this very fierce encounter Lance Corporal Keyworth stood fully exposed for 2 hours on top of the enemy parapet, and threw about 150 bombs amongst the Germans, who were only a few yards away.'

Keyworth had also been awarded the Medal of St George (2nd Class) Russian award. He died of his wounds on 19 October 1915 at the age of twenty-two. He is buried in the Abbeville Communal Cemetery in the Somme region of France. For most of the war the town of Abbeville was headquarters to the Commonwealth lines of communication, as well as a large medical facility, with both No.2 and No.5 Stationary Hospitals located there.

Lance Corporal Leonard James Keyworth VC.

Sergeant Alfred Joseph Knight of the 2nd/8th (City of London) Battalion, London Regiment (Post Office Rifles) holds the distinction of being the only Post Office Rifleman to be awarded the Victoria Cross. He won his award at Ypres on 20 September 1917 when his platoon came under heavy German machine gun fire. Single handedly and without any concern for his own personal safety, he rushed forward and captured the enemy position under continuous fire. He carried out several other acts of gallantry during the same period of fighting, in addition to taking charge of the battalion once all of the officers had been killed.

Lieutenant-Colonel Arthur Drummond Borton of the 2nd/22nd (County of London) Battalion, London Regiment was cited for the award of the Victoria Cross, in the *London Gazette,* 18 December 1917:

'In Sheria, Palestine, 7 November 1917,

Lance-Sergeant Alfred Joseph Knight, VC.

Lieutenant Colonel Arthur Drummond Borton DSO, of the 2nd/22nd (County of London) Battalion, London Regiment.

'For most conspicuous bravery and leadership in Sheria, Palestine. Under most difficult conditions in darkness and in an unknown country, he deployed his battalion for attack, and at dawn led his attacking companies against a strongly held position. When the leading waves were checked by a withering machine-gun fire, Lieutenant Colonel Borton showed an utter contempt of danger, and moved freely up and down his lines under heavy fire. Reorganising his command, he led his men forward, and captured the position.

'At a later stage of the fight, he led a party of volunteers against a battery of field guns in action at point-blank range, capturing the guns and the detachments. His fearless leadership was an inspiring example to the whole Brigade.'

Arthur Borton was invested with his Victoria Cross at Buckingham Palace on 23 February 1918, by George V.

The citation for his award of the Distinguished Service Order, seven months earlier, appeared in the *London Gazette*, on 31 May 1916, whilst he was serving with the Motor Machine-Gun Corps and the Royal Naval Air Service. It read as follows:

Lt-Col, Arthur Drummond Borton VC.

'In recognition of most valuable service whilst in command of a detachment of Royal Marine Motor Machine-Guns in difficult and dangerous parts of the line on the Gallipoli peninsula'.

Major Alexander Malins Lafone of the 1st County of London Yeomanry (Middlesex, Duke of Cambridge's Hussars). was forty-seven years of age when he was killed in action on 27 October 1917. He is buried at the Beersheba War Cemetery in Israel. The citation for the award of his Victoria Cross appeared in the *London Gazette* on 14 December 1917. It read as follows:

'For most conspicuous bravery, leadership, and self-sacrifice when holding a position for over seven hours against vastly superior enemy forces. All this time the enemy were shelling his position heavily, making it very difficult to see. In one attack, when the enemy cavalry charged his flank, he drove them back with heavy losses. In another charge they left fifteen casualties within twenty yards of his trench, one man, who reached the trench, being bayonetted by Major Lafone himself. When all his men, with the exception of three, had been hit and the trench which he was holding was so full of wounded that it was difficult to move and fire, he ordered those who

Major Alexander Malins Lafone, VC.

could walk to move to a trench slightly in the rear, and from his own position maintained a most heroic resistance. When finally surrounded and charged by the enemy, he stepped into the open and continued to fight until he was mortally wounded and fell unconscious. His cheerfulness and courage were a splendid inspiration to his men, and by his leadership and devotion he was enabled to maintain his position, which he had been ordered to hold at all costs.'

What makes this story even more remarkable is that Lafone should not have even been in the army let alone fighting such a rear guard action on the day he died. He had fought in the Second Boer War in South Africa and had been invalided out because of his wounds, in 1901. When the First World War began in 1914 he somehow managed to get himself back in to the army at the rank of major.

Temporary Lieutenant-Colonel Neville Elliot-Cooper (VC, DSO, MC) of the 8th Battalion, Royal Fusiliers, City of London Regiment. He was a career soldier having joined the army in 1908. He was 28 years old and the commanding officer of the 8th Battalion, The Royal Fusiliers, when he was awarded the Victoria Cross for his actions on 30 November

Lieutenant-Colonel Neville Elliot-Cooper, VC.

1917 during the battle of Cambrai. The citation for his award of the medal appeared in the *London Gazette* on 12 February 1918 and read as follows:

'For most conspicuous bravery and devotion to duty. Hearing that the enemy had broken through our outpost line, he rushed out of his dug-out, and on seeing them advancing across the open he mounted the parapet and dashed forward calling upon the Reserve Company and details of the Battalion Headquarters to follow. Absolutely unarmed, he made straight for the advancing enemy, and under his direction our men forced them back 600 yards. While still some forty yards in front he was severely wounded. Realizing that his men were greatly outnumbered and suffering heavy casualties, he signalled to them to withdraw, regardless of the fact that he himself must be taken prisoner. By his prompt and gallant leading he gained time for the reserves to move up and occupy the line of defence.'

He was taken prisoner by the Germans and died whilst in captivity at Hannover, Germany. He is buried in the Ohlsdorf Cemetery there.

Temporary Captain Robert Gee (VC, MC, MP) of the 2nd Battalion Royal Fusiliers, City of London Regiment had first joined the army in 1893 and by the time he had been awarded the Victoria Cross, he had served for twenty-four years. His moment of extreme bravery came on 30 November 1917 at Masnieres and Les Rues Vertes, France. The citation for his award read as follows:

Captain Robert Gee, VC.

'An attack by the enemy captured brigade headquarters and ammunition dump. Captain Gee, finding himself a prisoner, managed to escape and organized a party of the brigade staff with which he attacked the enemy, closely followed by two companies of infantry. He cleared the locality and established a defensive flank, then finding an enemy machine-gun still in action, with a revolver in each hand he went forward and captured the gun, killing eight of the crew. He was wounded, but would not have his wound dressed until the defence was organized.'

After the war Gee left the army and went into politics, becoming a Conservative MP.

Corporal Charles William Train, VC of the 2nd/14th (County of London) Battalion, London Regiment (London Scottish) was awarded the Victoria Cross for his actions on 8 December 1917 near Jerusalem. The citation for his award read as follows:

'On 8 December 1917 at Ein Kerem, near Jerusalem, in Ottoman controlled Palestine, when his company was unexpectedly engaged at close range by a party of the enemy with two machine guns and brought to a standstill, Corporal Train on his own initiative rushed forward and engaged the enemy with rifle grenades and succeeded in putting some of the team out of action by a direct hit. He shot and wounded an officer and killed or wounded the remainder of the team. After this he went to the assistance of a comrade who was bombing the enemy from the front and killed one of them who was carrying the second machine gun out of action.'

Corporal Charles William Train, VC.

Lance-Corporal John Alexander Christie of the 1st/11th Battalion, London Regiment (Finsbury Rifles) was only twenty-two years of age when he was awarded the Victoria Cross for his act of bravery.

'On 21 and 22 December 1917, at Fejja, Palestine, after a position had been captured, the enemy immediately made counter attacks up the communication trenches. Lance Corporal Christie, seeing what was happening, took a supply of bombs and went alone about 50 yards in the open along the communication trench and bombed the enemy. He continued to do this in spite of heavy opposition until a block had been established. On his way back he bombed more of the enemy who were

Lance Corporal John Alexander Christie, VC.

moving up the trench. His prompt action cleared a difficult position at a most difficult time and saved many lives.'

There is a plaque at Euston Railway station in London commemorating Lance Corporal Christie's actions and bravery at Fejja, which was unveiled by his son on 29 March 2014.

Lance-Corporal Charles Graham Robertson, VC, MM of the 10th Battalion, Royal Fusiliers was awarded the Victoria Cross for his act of bravery. The citation for his award read as follows:

'On 8 and 9 March 1918 west of Polderhoek Chateau, Belgium, Lance-Corporal Robertson having repelled a strong attack by the enemy, realised that he was being cut off and sent for reinforcements, while remaining at his post with only one man, firing his Lewis gun and killing large numbers of the enemy. No reinforcements arrived, so he withdrew, and then *Lance-Corporal* was forced to withdraw again to a defended post *Charles Graham* where he got on top of the parapet with a comrade, *Robertson, VC.* mounted his gun and continued firing. His comrade was almost immediately killed and he was severely wounded, but managed to crawl back with his gun, having exhausted his ammunition.'

He survived the war and served during the Second World War as a member of the Home Guard.

Acting Lieutenant-Colonel Oliver Cyril Spencer Watson, VC, DSO of the 1st County of London Yeomanry (Middlesex, Duke of Cambridge's Hussars), had first joined the army in 1897. He saw action during the Tirah Expedition on the North West Frontier during 1897 and 1898, when he was wounded. He next saw action during the Boxer Rebellion of 1900 and then again during the Second Boer War which finished in 1902, before being invalided home from India in 1903. The following year he left the army and was placed on the officers reserve list in 1904. He re-joined the Army in 1909, when he joined the County of London Yeomanry.

He was awarded the Victoria Cross for the following act of bravery whilst attached to the 2nd/5th Battalion, King's Own Yorkshire Light Infantry. This was reported in the *London Gazette*, dated 18 May 1918.

'On 28 March 1918 at Rossignol Wood, north of Hebuterne, France, a counter attack had been made against the enemy position which at first achieved its object, but as they were holding out in two improvised strong-points, Lieutenant-Colonel Watson saw that immediate action was necessary and he led his remaining small reserve to the attack, organising bombing

Acting Lieutenant-Colonel Oliver Cyril Spencer Watson.

parties and leading attacks under intense rifle and machine gunfire. Outnumbered, he finally ordered his men to retire, remaining himself in a communication trench to cover the retirement, though he faced almost certain death by so doing. The assault he led was at a critical moment and without doubt saved the line. Both in the assault and in covering his men's retirement, he held his life as nothing, and his splendid bravery inspired all his troops in the vicinity to rise to the occasion and save a breach being made in a hardly tried and attenuated line.'

Lt Col. Watson was killed covering the withdrawal. His body was never recovered so he has no known grave, but his name is commemorated on the Arras Memorial.

Private Robert Edward Cruickshank of the 4th Battalion, London Regiment was Canadian by birth, born in Winnipeg in 1888 but moved with his family to England in 1891.

Before the war he joined The City of London Yeomanry (Rough Riders), a volunteer unit with whom he served from 1908 to 1911. At the

Private Robert Edward Cruickshank

outbreak of the war he joined the Royal Flying Corps but transferred to the 14th (County of London) Battalion, London Regiment (London Scottish). He was wounded during the battle of the Somme and sent home to England to have his wounds treated and to recuperate. Once recovered he joined the fight again; this time he was sent to Egypt, which was where he would carry out the act of bravery that would define him for the rest of his days. On 1 May 1918 near to the River Jordan in Palestine he volunteered to take a message from his platoon, who were mostly wounded, officers and men alike, to the company headquarters. The following is the official War Office citation for the award of his Victoria Cross which was released on 21 June 1918.

'The platoon to which Private Cruickshank belonged came under heavy rifle and machine gun fire at short range and was led down a steep bank into a wadi, most of the men being hit before they reached the bottom. Immediately after reaching the bottom of the wadi the officer in command was shot dead, and the sergeant who then took over command sent a runner back to Company Headquarters asking for support, but was mortally wounded almost immediately after, the corporal having in the meantime been killed, the only remaining NCO (a Lance Corporal), believing the first messenger to have been killed, called a volunteer to take a second message back. Private Cruickshank immediately responded and rushed up the slope, but was hit and rolled back in to the wadi bottom. He again rose and rushed up the slope, but, being again wounded, rolled back in to the wadi. After his wounds had been dressed he rushed a third time up the slope and again fell badly wounded. Being now unable to stand he rolled himself back amid a hail of bullets. His wounds were now of such a nature as to preclude him making any further attempt and he lay all day in a dangerous position, being sniped at and again wounded here he lay. He displayed the utmost valour and endurance, and was cheerful and uncomplaining throughout.'

He was later evacuated back to England to have his wounds treated and to recuperate. Six months later on 24 October 1918 he received his Victoria Cross from George V at Buckingham Palace, with both his mother and fiancee, Gwendoline by his side.

Private Jack Harvey VC, of the 1st/22nd (County of London) Battalion, London Regiment (The Queens), was awarded the Victoria Cross for his actions on 2 September 1918. He was twenty-seven years of age at the time.

'On 2 September 1918, just north of Perone in France, when the advance of his company was held up by machine gun fire, Private Harvey dashed forward a distance of 50 yards alone, through the English barrage and in the face of heavy enemy fire. He rushed a machine gun post, shooting two of the team and bayoneting another. He then destroyed the gun and continued his way along the enemy trench. He single

Private Jack Harvey, VC.

handedly rushed an enemy dugout which contained 37 Germans and compelled them to surrender. These acts of gallantry saved the company heavy casualties and materially assisted in the success of the operation.'

1st/11th Battalion, London Regiment.

2nd/15th Battalion, London Regiment (Officers)

CHAPTER 6

Zeppelin and Gotha Raids on London

A Zeppelin was a type of airship which in essence consisted of a massive hydrogen filled balloon, with a number of manned gondolas located underneath the main body of the fuselage. They were the brain child of Count Ferdinand von Zeppelin, hence the name given to all such airships. Their design was first patented in France in 1895 and in 1910 they were flown and used commercially for the first time by Deutsche Luftschiffarts-AG (DELAG). It proved to be a successful venture, as between the time of its inaugural flight and the middle of 1914, just before the outbreak of war, the vessel had carried over 10,000 passengers on 1,500 flights.

Once the war had begun, Zeppelins were still used by both the German army and navy, but for military purposes, such as intelligence gathering and more notably, bombing raids over France as well as numerous towns and cities across England. During the war Germany built a total of eighty-four Zeppelins of which sixty were destroyed, as many by accident as at the hands of the British.

During the First World War a total of fifty-one bombing raids took place across the United Kingdom, in which a total of 5,806 bombs were dropped, resulting in the deaths of 557 civilians with a further 1358 people being injured. Germany used a total of 84 airships in these raids. Looked at in context, German Zeppelins flew over 1,000 patrols in the North Sea alone. They provided an excellent line of defence for

Germany against any naval attack from the Allies, even down to being able to see British vessels that were laying mines in German defended waters. At the start of the war the Kaiser had specifically ordered his country's Zeppelin commanders not to conduct any bombing raids over London or against buildings of an historic nature, Buckingham Palace being an obvious location.

A recruitment poster using Zeppelin Raids.

The first Zeppelin raid on England took place on the night of 19/20 January 1915, when two German airships, the L3 and L4 carried out raids along the east coast over Great Yarmouth, Sherringham and King's Lynn, killing four people and injuring a further sixteen in the process. Their intended target had actually been the Humberside coastline but they had been deterred from reaching the location by strong winds. Rather than return to Germany without having carried out any attacks, the east coast of England was a good alternative choice for them.

The Kaiser rescinded his order barring his Zeppelin commanders from not carrying out any attacks on England's capital city, and on 12 February 1915 he gave permission for his Zeppelins to bomb the London Docks, but notably, still not the very centre of London where the government and the Royal family were located as well as where Britain's gold reserves at the Bank of England could be found. Throughout April and May German Zeppelin raids had notably increased against targets along the east and south coasts of England.

The first actual Zeppelin raid on London during the war took place on 31 May 1915. The airship in question was LZ 38, which was commanded by German army officer, Linnarz. It carried out attacks over the Stoke Newington, Stepney and Leytonstone areas of London, dropping some 120 bombs in the process, which killed seven civilians and injured a further thirty-five. The resulting bombing caused widespread destruction to people's homes and businesses, as well as starting over forty fires.

The Daily Mirror on 2 June 1915 newspaper contained the following report.

Zeppelins drop 90 bombs in raid on London
Four persons killed, including a woman and an infant
Firemen needed at only three points –
Situation kept in hand by Police
Huns begin making excuses for latest crime.

'Official details issued yesterday of the Zeppelin raid on outlying parts of London show that about ninety bombs were dropped. The baby-killers will probably consider the object of their raid achieved, for one London infant is among the killed.With this innocent victim of frightfulness, a boy, a man and a woman make up the list of dead. Another woman was so badly injured that it is feared she cannot survive.The official statement issued yesterday supplemented an announcement which said, "Zeppelins are reported to have been seen near Ramsgate and Brentwood and in certain outlying districts of London." Already the Germans are trying to make some excuse for the murder of helpless non-combatants. Last night's Berlin official report says; As a result of a bombardment of the open town of Ludwigshafen we last night threw numerous bombs on the wharves and docks of London. This reprisal excuse is a typical German perversion of the facts. The French raid on the big explosives factory at Ludwigshafen, on the Rhine, was made last Thursday as a retaliation for the bombs dropped on Paris by Taubes.'

Such reports are always fascinating to read, giving a real flavour of the time and the outrage that was felt as a result of the Zeppelin raid. People were so incensed by what had happened and shocked that it had taken place in London, it led to riots in the capital later the same day, most of the anger being aimed at German shops and properties in the area.

In June 1915, the summer months brought with them the added danger for German Zeppelin crews of long bright evenings, so Germany took the opportunity to send her fleet of army Zeppelins to assist her troops who were fighting the Russians on the Eastern front, with the naval airships remaining in place to be able carry on their attacks on England as soon as the opportunity arose.

The first attempt by the German navy to carry out a Zeppelin raid on London took place on 4 June 1915. It was carried out by L 9, but because of strong winds in the English Channel, the ship's commander misjudged his position and ended up dropping his bombs over Gravesend in Kent. Not to be put off, two days later the L 9 was back to try her luck again, but was once again beaten by the weather and ended up dropping her bombs over Hull, on the North-east coast of England, instead of London. The same evening saw three army Zeppelins which were also on route to London, having to turn back to their base at Evere in Belgium, brought about because of bad weather. The evening was not to be a totally uneventful one for the Zeppelins; as they neared their base they ran into aircraft from the British Royal Naval Air Service (RNAS), who were flying out of their base at Furnes in Belgium. The LZ 38 was destroyed on the ground, whilst its sister ship, the LZ 37 was brought down by twenty-three year old Sub-Lieutenant Reginald Alexander John Warneford, who was flying a Morane-Saulnier Type L aircraft. For his actions that day he was awarded both the Victoria Cross, by the British and the Legion d'honneur. by the French. On the same day that he received his Legion d'honneur from the Commander in Chief, General Joffre, the aircraft he was flying in, with an American journalist, fell apart and crashed to the ground. Warneford died on his way to hospital. The crews of both the LZ 37 and LZ 38, all perished. As a result of this incident, both the German army and German navy withdrew their Zeppelins from Belgium.

After an attack on Tyneside on the evening of 15/16 June 1915, by the navy Zeppelin, L10, further raids on England were halted for two months because of the long, light summer evenings.

On the night of 17/18 August the L10 became the first navy Zeppelin to actually reach London, and carry out an attack, dropping its deadly cargo of bombs over Walthamstow and Leytonstone, rather than the centre of London as had been intended, because of mistakes by its commander on being unable to correctly identify land markings. Two weeks later the L 10 was struck by lightning off Cuxhaven, in Lower Saxony, Germany; it caught fire and crashed, killing all of its crew .

There were no reports whatsoever in the *Daily Mirror* about this incident in the days after it happened. As far as the Mirror was concerned it was incident that simply did not take place. However, in the *Yorkshire Telegraph and Star* evening dated Wednesday 18 August the following article appeared.

Another Air Raid
Ten civilians killed and thirty-six injured
Eastern Counties visited.

'Another air raid by Zeppelins was announced by the Press Bureau this afternoon. Last night enemy airships visited the Eastern Counties and dropped bombs which killed seven men, two women and a child, while thirty-six persons were injured. All were civilians. Damage was done to a church and other buildings. One of the airships is believed to have been hit by our anti-aircraft guns, but all the raiders made good their escape,'

It is odd that a report of a Zeppelin raid on England's capital city is not reported in a major daily newspaper, but does appear in the *Yorkshire Telegraph* even though there is no mention of the target city.

On 7 September 1915, the German Zeppelin SL 2, commanded by Haptmann Von Wobeser, dropped six bombs over the Millwall, New Cross and Deptford areas of London. By the time the raid was over, sixteen people had been killed and at least another twenty injured. LZ 74, which had been on a bombing raid over Cheshunt in Hertfordshire, where she had dropped thirty-nine bombs, was making her way back home when she dropped just one bomb whilst flying over London, which landed on Fenchurch Street railway station.

Plaque at 61 Farringdon Road.

The following evening, 8 September saw London attacked once again, this time by Zeppelin L 13, which was commanded by Kapitanleutnant Heinrich Mathy. He proceeded to drop bombs close to Smithfield meat market, killing two men and destroying several houses in the process. The attack continued less than a mile away when a number of bombs were dropped close to St Paul's Cathedral, landing on a number of textile warehouses, causing a fire of such magnitude that it took twenty-two fire engines to extinguish the flames. The Zeppelin's next target, intended or otherwise, was Liverpool Street Railway station, where she dropped the remainder of her bombs before making good her escape. By the time the raid was over, twenty-two civilians were dead and another eighty-seven were injured as well as damage to homes and businesses running in to tens of thousands of pounds. Despite valiant efforts from anti-aircraft crews on the ground, the L 13 escaped unscathed.

The following report appeared in the *Daily Mirror* on Friday 10 September

20 killed and 86 injured in the raid on London and East Coast
Fire bombs dropped in London area

'Another Zeppelin raid, this time on the Eastern Counties and the London District was announced yesterday to have taken place during the previous night. Bombs, both explosive and incendiary, were dropped, and some fires were caused. The outbreaks being, however, got well under control by midnight. The total of casualties amounted to 106, twenty being killed, of whom two were women and six were children. Only four soldiers were hurt, one being killed and three being injured. Berlin's version of the same raid was as follows; "German Zeppelins dropped bombs on the western part of the City of London, on some large factories near Norwich and on the harbour works and iron works at Middlesbrough. All the airships returned safely."'

When reading the article in the newspaper, one cannot help feeling that there was an orchestrated attempt by the authorities to play down what happened through fear of affecting the public's morale. Twenty civilians were killed and another eighty-six injured on English soil, yet it only warrants twenty-two lines on page three of a national newspaper.

On 13 October the L 15, which was one of five Zeppelins launched from their home base by the German Navy, dropped her 'pay load' over the area of Charing Cross in London, with one of the bombs striking the Lyceum Theatre. A total of seventeen people were killed in the attack with another twenty injured. None of the bombs fell within the City of London and none of the four other Zeppelins which were part of the same raid, managed to reach London. This would prove to be the last Zeppelin raid on London in 1915. Although one of the bombs dropped by L 15 landed on an army camp in Folkestone, Kent, this was undoubtedly not its intended target, and the raid had no other real significant military purpose. Each and every raid did however bring the war to the 'front doors' of the British people, causing, fear and trepidation amongst their ranks.

The following article appeared in the *Daily Mirror* on Thursday 14 October 1915.

Zeppelin raid on London area last night.
Incendiary and explosive bombs dropped by foe aircraft.
8 persons killed and 34 injured.
Small damage done. No public building injured,
and few fires caused.
Dead include two women and one soldier.

'A Zeppelin raid over a portion of the London area was made last night. No public buildings were damaged but two men and six women were killed and about thirty-four people were injured These were the casualties reported at 11.45 pm. A statement will be issued by the Admiralty today when further particulars are available.'

This time the report was on page five of the newspaper and warranted only very basic details contained in twelve lines.

The Zeppelin raids were an interesting factor of the war as they had absolutely no real impact from a military perspective. They had not killed tens of thousands of young soldiers waiting to go and fight on the Western Front; they had not sunk any British vessels, making the

English Channel a safer place for their own submarines; and they had not destroyed vast numbers of British aircraft. What they had done though was badly affect British public morale making the civilian population feel vulnerable and threatened. It greatly raised the misplaced belief in the minds of the masses that the Zeppelin raids were a precursor to a full scale land invasion

By the time the raids had recommenced in 1916, the British had improved their coastal ground defences and brought in high powered search lights so as to be able to more easily locate attacking Zeppelins. Germany had not exactly been idle during the same period. She had focused her efforts on improving her fleet of Zeppelins, bringing in the new Q class airships, which were not only bigger but could bomb from a greater height than the P class had previously been able to do. Although the Germans had continued their Zeppelin raids across England throughout 1916, they had left London alone, possibly because of the increased and improved defensive positions placed in around London and across the south coast. More often than not the raids failed to even reach their intended targets, either settling for a secondary location, or being forced to turn back because of poor weather conditions. Throughout the war bad weather was most probably the City of London's biggest defensive weapon, preventing or redirecting numerous intended Zeppelin raids.

On the evening of 24/25 August 1916 a German Zeppelin, the L 31, one of the new and much larger R class airships, commanded by Heinrich Mathy, dropped a total of thirty-six bombs over the Deptford area of London. As a result of the attack nine people were killed and forty more were injured.

On Friday 25 August 1916 the following report appeared in the *Dover Express,*

Zeppelin raids last night.
Attacks on East and South East coasts by several Airships.

'The following official report was issued by Lord French at one o'clock this morning; Several airships crossed the East and South East Coasts of England shortly before midnight. A number of bombs were dropped. So far no reports of any casualty or damage has yet been received. War Office, Thursday, 11.50 am.;

One hostile airship crossed the East Coast shortly before midnight. A number of incendiary and explosive bombs were dropped in open fields.No damage and no casualties have been reported. The airship went to sea again before 1 am.'

The two officially released reports of the incident were different even though nine people were actually killed during the bombings with another forty being injured. Yet again this was not front page news as might possibly be expected of such an incident, instead it was on page five of an eight page newspaper and consisted of fifteen lines of print. The same day a similar report appeared in the *Sunderland Daily Echo* and *Shipping Gazette*. It contained a bit more detail, although in essence it was from the same sources as those that were used in the Dover Express report, yet it contained thirty-seven lines and it was on the back page of a six page newspaper.

The evening of 2/3 September 1916 saw a combined German army and navy raid of sixteen Zeppelins take place in a coordinated attack over England with the intended target being London. Unfortunately for the Germans the weather was extremely bad in the North Sea, on the night they had chosen to carry out their latest attack. There was heavy rain as well as snowstorms, which was not particularly good news for any type of aircraft, especially a Zeppelin. Out of the original sixteen airships, only one of them, the SL 11, managed to get anywhere near London. As it headed towards its target it flew over Hertfordshire and then on to Ponders End in North London where it dropped some of its bombs. Luck was not on its side and it was picked up by searchlight units on the ground. At just after 2 am on 3 September 1916, the SL 11 was spotted by Lieutenant William Leefe Robinson of the Royal Flying Corps, flying a BE 2 single engine, two seater biplane. Lieutenant Robinson opened fire on the Zeppelin, letting off three drums of ammunition into the cornered airship. The first drum had no effect at all, neither did the second, but the third most certainly did. It set the Zeppelin on fire and the stricken airship quickly burst into a ball of flame before crashing to the ground near Cuffley in Hertfordshire. All of the crew perished in the flames. For his actions that evening, Lieutenant William Leefe Robinson was awarded the Victoria Cross and a purse of more than £3,500, collected from a grateful public, a staggering sum of money at the time.

The *Sunderland Daily Echo* and *Shipping Gazette* of Monday 25 September 1916 reported the following;

'The Germans had threatened some days ago that before the end of September they would make a 'devastating' attack on London. From Saturday midnight till 2 am yesterday the 12 Zeppelins which came over the cruised about Lincolnshire, the East Midlands and South Eastern Counties and the Eastern and South Eastern suburbs of London. Many bombs were dropped. Most of these fell in the sea or in places where they did no harm. The rest, unfortunately, were dropped in inhabited areas, with the result that the casualties were regrettably heavy. In London 17 men, 8 women and 3 children were killed whilst 45 men, 37 women and 17 children were injured, out of a total of 32 people who were killed and 110 who were injured across the country as part of the same raid.

'It is noted that one of the London intruders lowered a powerful light, which illuminated the district, and then a shower of bombs fell.'

'On the night of 23/24 September 1916 a total of twelve Zeppelins were involved in a wide spread attack all over the country, including the North East of England, the Midlands and the South East. L 31 made it in to London and dropped its bombs on the unsuspecting folk of Leyton, killing eight people and injuring thirty. This was the same night that saw two Zeppelins shot down over Essex, the L 32 over Great Burstead which resulted in the loss of her entire crew, and the L 33 which was brought down by anti-aircraft fire, and crash landed at Little Wigborough. All but one of her crew survived, who then set fire to the airship to stop her falling in to the hands of the British.'

In the same newspaper was the following report of a British soldier.

Tragedy of a Soldier

'One particular tragic case is reported form a London suburb. A soldier who had obtained special leave from the front to visit his father, who was dying, was expected to reach home on Saturday evening. Some delay however, prevented his reaching his father's house until yesterday morning, only to find the place in ruins, his father having been killed outright and his mother and sister lying unconscious in hospital seriously injured.

'The poor fellow scrambled in amongst the ruins of what was once his home. For a few moments he gazed about him pitifully, and then, bursting into tears, he flung himself down amid the debris and sobbed unrestrainedly until another soldier approached him, and laying his hand on the man's shoulder, begged him to calm himself. Scrambling to his feet the soldier shook his fist savagely in the air.

'"My God,' he exclaimed, 'wait until I get back to the front again. The devils shall pay for this."'

The London Guarantee and Accident Company Limited of Leeds, had spotted a gap in the insurance market, and so it was that on Thursday 28 September 1916 that they took out an advertisement in the Yorkshire Evening Post pointing out that personal injuries due to aircraft were not covered by an ordinary Personal Accident Policy. It said the following;

'Leeds Branch, 1 East Parade, Leeds, will grant a policy to any British subject of either sex between the ages of 12 and 70 whilst resident in the United Kingdom of Great Britain and Ireland against Death or Injury directly caused by Aircraft (Hostile or otherwise), including bombes, shells and or missiles dropped or thrown therefrom or fired thereat, on the following terms.
　　　5/- for SIX MONTHS
　　　7/6 for TWELVE MONTHS
　　　10/- for the Duration of the War.'

The Benefits section was where it became slightly surreal even though it was a completely serious advert;

'Benefits
£500 payable in the event of death.
£500 payable in the event of the loss of Two Limbs or Two
　　　 Eyes.

£250 payable in the event of the loss of One Limb or One Eye.

£2   per week payable during Temporary Total Disablement, for a period not exceeding 13 weeks.'

The last raid on London of 1916 took place on 1 October. Although eleven Zeppelins set out on the raid only one actually made it through. The L 31, being flown by the experienced Kapitan, Heinrich Mathy, who was making his fifteenth raid,. Sadly for him, it would also be his last. As L 31 was flying over Cheshunt it was picked up by the powerful searchlight batteries, which clearly illuminated it in the night sky for all to see, which included three aircraft from No. 39 Squadron, RFC, one of which was being flown by 2nd Lieutenant Wulstan Tempest. He attacked the ship with all guns blazing, quickly managing to set the stricken aircraft on fire. It sank to the ground in the Cheshunt area with the loss of all those on board, some of the crew taking the decision to jump to their deaths rather than die a potentially slow and agonising death in the flames.

It would be more than a year before the next attack on the capital, which would also be the last attack on London by a Zeppelin. On the night of 19/20 October 1917 L 45 carried out a raid on London dropping three bombs in Piccadilly, Camberwell and in Glenview Road, Hither Green. Three houses were totally destroyed in the attack and many more were badly damaged. Fifteen civilians were killed including seven children of the Kingston family and four more from the Millgate family. The night did not end well for L 45, after leaving London she encountered mechanical problems in three of her engines and despite losing altitude she was blown by the winds back to France where she eventually came down near a town called Sisteron, situated in the Alps Cote d'azur region. If she had continued on much further she would have ended up in the Mediterranean. Her crew, who all survived, set fire to her before surrendering.

Prior to this Germany had intended to carry out two Zeppelin raids on London, but on neither occasion did any of the airships reach their intended target. On 16 March 1917, five Zeppelins set off to attack the City but after encountering very strong winds, collectively made the decision to return home. One of them, the L 39, found itself over French territory and was shot down by ground fire. On 23 May 1917 the Germans tried again; on this occasion they sent six Zeppelins to raid London, but were once again defeated by the weather, a combination of high winds and thick cloud. A few bombs were dropped on Suffolk, on England's east coast, before they returned home.

On Saturday 20 October 1917 the following report appeared in the Yorkshire Evening Post

The most silent attack on record.
Casualties in London area.

'Everybody here is agreed that last night's raid was the most silent on record, for no anti-aircraft gun appears to have come into action. Until bombs fell few people had the faintest of ideas that a hostile airship was overhead. The following facts have been collected, which summarise the results of the raid so far as the London area is concerned. Three bombs were dropped, 21 persons were killed and 13 injured. Four people were killed in one centre. Twelve persons were killed and nine injured and three houses demolished in another district. Five persons were killed and four injured and two shops and a house demolished in a third district. In connection with the work of rescue mention must be made of the heroic action of a sailor on leave, who, coming to the scene of an explosion within two or three minutes of the bomb falling, stripped to the waist and working for nine hours without a break, digging out the bodies and helping the wounded to the ambulances. The body of a little girl had not been recovered up to a late hour today. The projectile is thought to have been an aerial torpedo.

'One bomb in the London area killed 11 people. A bomb which fell in a London street killed five passers-by. An aerial torpedo fell in the centre of a street. It exploded with a tremendous detonation, and the windows of an adjacent shop were completely wrecked. Practically every large window within one hundred yards was either smashed or badly cracked. A Policeman on duty in the vicinity had his helmet blown off.'

The report mentioned that nobody had heard or knew that the Zeppelins were overhead, including the anti-aircraft batteries, none of which opened up on their unseen enemy. This could possibly have been because of the higher altitude at which the newer, S-Class Zeppelins, could now operate. This was 16,500 feet, with a maximum ceiling of a staggering 21,000. This new height was dangerous not just for the unsuspecting British public, but for the Zeppelin crews as well. Flying at such heights meant having to contend with extreme cold, high winds as well as altitude sickness.

Besides Zeppelins, Germany also had Gotha airplanes that could cross the English Channel and attack British towns and cities. The Gotha G lV, to give the aircraft its full name, was a bi-plane and heavy bomber, the first of its kind, which was operated by the Imperial German Air Service, or Luftstreitkraffe. The aircraft was a truly devastating machine for its time. It had a two

Zeppelin Fund Poster by the Daily Mail.

man crew of a pilot and a bombardier as well as an arsenal which allowed for a maximum of four machine guns. The first Gotha G LV

Members of Kaghohl 3 with a Gotha aircraft 1917.

came into service in March 1917 in readiness for Operation Turkenkreuz, which was a planned, strategic bombing of London.

The first Gotha aircraft raid on England during the First World War was not on London, but still deserves a mention. It was 25 May 1917 when a total of twenty-three Gotha heavy bombers set out to raid targets across southeast England. Only two of the bombers reached their intended targets, killing 95 people and injuring 192. This included both soldiers and civilians. The first of the Gotha aircraft raids on London took place on 12 June. This would be the first of twenty-seven such raids over London between then and the end of the war. Fourteen Gotha bombers were involved in the raid which saw more than 100 bombs dropped. The effect on the ground was devastating with a total of 162 civilians killed, making it the capital's highest death toll of the war. On 31 October incendiary bombs were dropped on London for the first time during a raid by twenty-two Gothas, killing ten civilians.

There was another raid on London on the evening of 28 January 1918, carried out by three Gotha aircraft, one of which was brought down over Essex by two aircraft from the Royal Flying Corps. The two British pilots who shot down the Gotha were Captain G H Hackwill, who had previously served with the Somerset Light Infantry and Lieutenant C C Banks, who had previously served with the Welsh Fusiliers.

An eye witness account of the incident was as follows.

'One Gotha, apparently lame, banged and bumped her way homewards in apparent safety, until the moon showed her up against the background of the sky. 'Archies' roared out at her, the face of the moon was covered with little smoke clouds, and the Gotha turned from the barrage, wheeled in the sky, and droned on, only to meet more guns. Then the guns ceased again and gave way to the machine gun cackle, and suddenly the raider turned over and came down in flames.' The three man crew of the German Gotha all perished in the crash.

As well as Gotha aircraft the Germans also used Zeppelin-Staaken Riesenflugzeug 'Giant' bombers in their raids on England. They were literarily giant planes. Their wingspan was a massive 138 feet and they could carry a maximum 4,400lb bomb load, although the longer the

Members of the Army and RFC inspect the crashed Gotha.

flight was then the less weight the aircraft could carry, which was rather fortunate for England. Ironically it was because of concerns by the British authorities over their defences against German Zeppelins and other aircraft such as the Gothas and the Zeppelin-Staaken Giant bombers that the Royal Air Force came into being on 1 April 1918. Prior to this Britain's defences had been the joint responsibility of the Admiralty who had flight capability with the Royal Naval Air Service, and the army's, Royal Flying Corps. The Government set in place a Parliamentary Inquiry under the control of Jan Smuts, who was the Commander of the South African forces during the First World War, and was also a member of the British War Cabinet between 1917 and 1919.

On the night of 16 February 1918 four Zeppelin-Staaken giant bombers set course for England, with their intended target being London. During the raid, one of the German aircraft dropped a bomb which weighed 2,200lb, which as it transpired, was the largest ever dropped during the course of the war by either side. It landed on Chelsea hospital, blowing up an entire wing in the process. The following evening saw a single Zeppelin-Staaken bomber, braving the English defences and making its way to London where it dropped a bomb on St Pancras railway station, causing massive damage. Twenty-eight Gothas set out on another raid on 19 May 1918, their intended target, London. The result was the death of forty-eight civilians. Six of the Gotha bombers were shot down by British aircraft from the newly formed Royal Air Force. This would be the last German aerial attack on England during the First World War.

It was at about this time that a defensive ring of Barrage Balloons were set up around London to prevent German aerial attacks on the capital, Germany lost sixty-one of their Gotha aircraft between September 1917 and May 1918, during raids on England. It is debatable as to the effectiveness of Germany's Operation Turkenreuz. Its major success was undoubtedly the fear it managed to instil in the minds of the British public, especially those who lived in the Southern part of the country across Kent, Essex, Suffolk, Norfolk, Hertfordshire and London. It also achieved the need by the British authorities to allocate 12 squadrons of aircraft and some 10,000 servicemen to the defence of Britain, men and machines that no doubt would have been extremely helpful to the fighting across the Western Front, and other theatres of war, but needs must.

CHAPTER 7

St Bartholomew's Hospital Women at Work and FANY's

St Bartholomew's, or St Barts as it is also affectionately known, is the oldest hospital in Europe having first been founded in 1123; it still remains on its original site at Smithfield, and is the only hospital that falls within the City of London.

Over the years, St Bartholomew's hospital has seen, and been the centre of some of the major advancements in the medical field, which at times has seen slow progression. As recently as the late eighteen hundreds, the actual trauma of an operation and postoperative infection were still amongst the greatest causes of death in hospital patients.

During the First World War the East Wing of St Bart's Hospital was used to treat wounded British soldiers. There is a memorial tablet on the north wall of the hospital in memory of the men who were treated there. The inscription reads as follows.

'This inscription records the fact that this wing of the hospital was placed at the service of the War Office during the Great War and was occupied by sick and wounded soldiers of the British

Memorial to soldiers treated at the hospital during the war.

Expeditionary Forces from October 1914 until the 31st January 1919. 5406 soldiers were passed through the wards.'

Even though the war didn't begin until August 1914, the threat of war had prevailed for many years, to such an extent that the War Office had been making preparations to ensure that it had sufficient nursing staff in place when the inevitable happened. A letter dated 7 March 1911 was sent by the Matron-in-Chief of the Queen Alexandria's Imperial Military Nursing Service (QAIMNS) at the War Office to St Bartholomew's Hospital.

'Reserve of Nurses for Queen Alexandra's Imperial Military Nursing Service
'Dear Madam,
'With reference to your reply dated January 27 to the letter on the above subject from the Director General of the Army Medical Services, it is fully recognised that great demands have already been made on the Civil Hospitals, which have been most liberally met.

'We would, however, ask your kind consideration of this further proposal, that, when calculating the number of nurses you can recommend, your committee do promise to the War Office to augment Queen Alexandra's Imperial Military Nursing Service in time of war, you will include any you may have trained, and know to be in every way suitable although they are no longer working in your hospital. It is felt in this way we may rely upon getting efficient and reliable nurses and at the same time cause less inconvenience to the matrons of civil hospitals.

Thanking you for your kind interest in this matter.

I am Madam,

Yours very truly

Matron-in-Chief

QAIMNS.'

During the First World War there was a Territorial Force Nursing Service Hospital situated at Camberwell in London, which was located in what was a former missionary college. A lot of the nurses who treated British and Allied soldiers at the hospital were from St Bart's. Looking back in history, it is clear that conflicts such as the First World War, led directly to advancements in the medical world, as doctors and surgeons had to suddenly find new ways of treating wounds that they had not previously had to deal with.

A source of excellent information concerning members of staff from St Bartholomew's Hospital was their monthly newspaper *Journal*. It carried numerous articles about interesting medical matters, as well as specific information about its own members of staff, particularly those who had enlisted in the armed forces to do their bit for king and country. It covered such matters as gallantry awards, promotions and sadly, deaths as well.

The first issue of the *Journal* which came out after the outbreak of war, was in September 1914. Understandably, the editorial notes of that month's issue were all about the war. It was clear from its tone that the war had always been expected rather than if it would happen. Even though it had been years in the coming, when it did, its apparent suddenness seemed to have caught everyone slightly by surprise.

With the war finally upon them for real, staff from the hospital clearly wanted to do their bit; whilst others amongst them, who viewed the war from a slightly wider perspective, called for caution. This was not out of any disloyalty but rather common sense. The concern was that, with everybody keen and eager to rush off to the different theatres of war to do their bit, that there would be nobody left behind to care for the sick and infirm who came through the hospital's front doors every single day. Just because there was a war on, people didn't suddenly stop being sick back home. It was a real dilemma for the medical profession to have to contemplate, as well as the hospital's governing body. There was no doubting that everybody would be called upon to serve their country, one way or another; but how and where individuals did so, some felt, had to be given careful consideration.

St Bartholomew's hospital had already been mobilized to support the war effort by September 1914. They were attached to a Territorial Base Hospital, known as the First London (City of London) General Hospital, which was based at St Gabriel's Training College, near Camberwell New Road. It was staffed by doctors, nurses and orderlies from St Bart's and came under the command of Colonel W A Atkinson of the Royal Army Medical Corps, Territorial Force. A group of some ninety nurses from current and previous St Bart's staff, were also allocated to the mobilized hospital. The hospital also made a further one hundred of its nurses available to the Admiralty, the War Office as well as other military hospitals.

At the outbreak of the war the governors of St Bartholomew's hospital decided to place the hospital's East Wing, which consisted of 198 beds, at the service of the war office, specifically for the care and treatment of wounded and sick British and Allied soldiers. The wing was up and running by the beginning of September. At the very start of the war fifteen members of staff, most likely doctors, along with thirty of the hospital's students, all enlisted for active service such was their desire and commitment to do their bit.

The issues of the *Journal* throughout the war years carried similar topics month to month; Editor's notes, calendar, from the front, medical notes and correspondence being the usual headings.

The issue dated 1 October 1917 mentioned how Captain J A Bell of the Royal Army Medical Corps, who prior to going off to war, worked at St Bartholomew's Hospital, was awarded the Military Cross.

The East Wing at St Bartholomew's Hospital.

'During a heavy bombardment, he proceeded along a road which was exposed to the most intense shell fire in order to attend four wounded officers. He dressed their wounds and remained with them until they were evacuated by motor ambulance, which was only accomplished with the greatest of difficulty owing to the heavy shelling. His absolute disregard of danger and devotion to duty amidst terrific shell fire were exceptionally splendid and beyond all praise.'

In the same issue the deaths of two of St Bartholomew's recently qualified students was reported.

'Captain B A Bull, RAMC, was killed in action on September 16th. He took a temporary commission in the RAMC last year, and was promoted Captain after a year's service.
'Temp. Surg. J D Rutherford, RN, HMS Theseus, died from tuberculosis of the lungs on HM Hospital Ship Karapara on September 13th in the East Mediterranean very shortly after his entry into the Navy.

Our very sincere sympathy is extended to the parents and relatives of these two late fellow students of ours.'

In the same issue was the report of the death of Captain Harris RAMC who was attached to the Royal Field Artillery, who was killed in action on 31 July 1917.

The issue dated 1 November 1917 included the following news about the deaths in the war of three of its members of staff. Lieutenant R Gordon Hill, MC, RAMC, of the Coldstream Guards, and a married man, was killed in action on 11 October 1917. His widow, Ivy, lived in Purley, London. Captain Reginald Sherman of the RAMC had been serving with a Field Ambulance unit when he died of his wounds on 10 October 1917. He was a married man who left behind a widow, Dorothy. Captain John Beaufoy Randall, RAMC, who was twenty-eight years of age, was killed in action on 31 October 1917.

In the continually rising number of men included on the hospitals Roll of Honour, the issue of the *Journal*, dated 1 December 1917, reports the death of another previous student who was killed in the service of his country.

'It is with deep regret that we hear of the death of Lieut. L E Forman, who was previously a student at this hospital. He obtained a commission in the RNAS, on July 28th, 1917, and was killed in an accident whilst flying on August 16th. We extend our heartfelt sympathy to his relatives and friends.'

An interesting aspect of the content of the Journals was the correspondence page, which produced some interesting letters to the editor. In particular were the ones that were sent in from doctors in the military, usually from either the Royal Army Medical Corps or the Army Medical Service, who were serving in France and other theatres of war. Quite often they were able to provide knowledge of their first hand experiences dealing with a variety of wounds and diseases that before the war were in some cases no more than theories or beliefs.

Hospitals in pre-war times were very structured places, where there was a set way of dealing with matters and doing things; but quite often in the aftermath of a bloody and gruesome battle, how to treat some of the wounds that soldiers had sustained were not to be found in the pages of any instruction manual. Doctors had to learn quickly how to be flexible in their approach and to be able to 'think outside of the box' to deal effectively with the wounds they saw.

The issue of the Journal for December 1918 was a varied and interesting edition as might be expected for the first one of a new era in post war Great Britain. It spoke of some ex-members of staff at the hospital who sadly had not made it through the war.

'Capt. R Brewitt-Taylor, MC, RAMC, was killed in France by a shell on August 22nd, 1918, when he was on his way to the front line with his stretcher bearers. Capt, Brewitt-Taylor left England for France in August 1914. He served as the Regimental Medical Officer through 1915, was in Mesopotamia in 1916, and in France again during 1917-18. At the time of his death, he was attached to the 7th Field Ambulance.

'Surg. Sub-Lieutenant T Carlyle, RNVR, died of pneumonia in St Bartholomew's hospital on October 21st, 1918, aged 24. He entered the hospital in October 1913. He volunteered as a probationary surgeon two years ago, and only returned to the hospital last month.

'Capt. James Harris Connolly, RAMC, died at Acheson Military Hospital, Regents Park, London, on October 23rd, 1918 aged 42. He took a temporary commission as a Lieutenant in the RAMC on October 10th, 1914, and was promoted Captain after a year's service.

'Surgeon-Lieutenant Commander John Hadwen R N, died in service on November 2nd 1918. In the early part of the war, he served on board HMS King Edward Vll.

'Capt. Walter Malden, RAMC (TF) died at Cambridge on October 28th, 1918 Aged 60. He took a commission as a Captain in the RAMC (TF) on the staff of the 1st Eastern (Cambridge) General Hospital on May 6th 1908, as a pathologist.'

In the correspondence section of the *Journal*, was a letter from an un-named British major who was serving with the RAMC with the British Expeditionary Force and wanted to have his say about the viability of starting up a National Medical Service after the war, utilising those who served in the Royal Army Medical Service.

His observations were based on the amount of wounded and sick soldiers the RAMC dealt with throughout the war, efficiently and quickly, and the belief that if such medical care could be made to work for wounded soldiers, then why not for an entire civilian population. The writer of the letter could only see positives for such a ground breaking move, stating that as so much had been learnt medically as a result of the war, it would be morally wrong to not let everybody benefit from the new medical procedures which had come about as a result of it, arguing that it would be good for the patients, good for the medical profession and especially for the advancement of medical knowledge.

Little did he know that he was describing the National Health Service, or that his idea would eventually come to fruition; but sadly, not for another thirty years.

In 1949, Constance (Emma) Wilson, who had been a nurse at St Bartholomew's Hospital during the war, wrote a brief autobiography entitled, *Those Were The Days*, which she dedicated to all Minto Sisters. Some of it was about her time spent at St Bartholomew's hospital. Below are some extracts from it:

'During 1915 I applied to St Bartholomew's Hospital London,

for a vacancy, but was turned down as an unsuitable candidate in that I appeared too delicate for such heavy work. Those hated spots still covered my face and were, no doubt, largely responsible for the decision. With some pulling of strings, and more determination, I tried again after six months, and to my great joy, was accepted. The Matron made it quite clear at the second interview that she looked upon me as an unsuitable candidate but must accept the decision of the Medical Board, and she rubbed it well in that if, for any reason, I became sick and had to go off duty during my first year of training, she would not hesitate to ask me to leave, and no second chance could be given. This, more than ever, made me determined to stick it out, and not until my third year at Barts, just before my final exam, did I have to report sick and go off duty with influenza during the 1918 epidemic. This was my only spell off duty on account of sickness.

'In May 1916 my training commenced. Duly dressed up in a monstrously long grey dress (which was soon shortened) according to regulations, white apron, collar and cap, I timidly entered one of the women's surgical wards and reported to the Sister. The words that greeted my appearance were enough to daunt the ardour of the bravest new probationer. "Now who on earth are you," said Sister, "we are far too busy to be bothered with any new probationers today. I cannot think what Matron is thinking of. Look at this bright specimen, Nurse, she looks as though she needed to be warded herself. What can we do with her?"

'The Blue Belt (fourth year nurse) joined the Sister and had a look at me. Meekly looking up into the hard steely blue eyes of the old Sister, I remained mute, thereby adding to her irritation.

"Can you give bedpans?" asked the Nurse.

"Oh yes," I replied thankfully, "I have been a VAD."

"I advise you to keep that quiet," snapped the Sister. "We do not want any VAD's here, thinking they know everything, stupid useless creatures. The less you remember about that shady part of your life, the better. Now go along and get out of my sight; give every patient a bedpan, and heaven protect them."

'Proudly I marched down the ward into the sluice room. Here

I was at home, batting on my own ground, I knew what to do, and the presentation of bed pans to some sixteen to twenty women kept me busily employed and helped me to find my sea legs, so to speak.

'Life was hard, cleaning, washing patients, making beds, giving bedpans and then, cleaning again. All day and every day, lockers, brasses, cupboards, bed ends, bathrooms, sluices, macintoshes and spittoons. Very seldom was anything of interest or of a constructive nature shown to us probationers. We learned through our mistakes and failures. Poor patients! It was during this first year that I acquired my sense of humour I think, which was to stand me in good stead on many future occasions. Fortified; too, with the knowledge, sound or otherwise, of my VAD training; with this help, meagre as it was, at my back, somehow or other I came through.

'How I survived that first year I just do not know, I doggedly stayed on duty looking like a ghost, or as my colleagues often remarked, like a perforated gastric; sometimes it was a slight temperature and headache, but mostly just a feeling of utter tiredness. I made myself play tennis in the summer months during my off duty and I gritted my teeth and remembered Matron's warning, becoming more and more determined that nothing short of death would make me give in.

'Somehow or other I came through the first year. Many fell by the way, as often as not, because of the sting and biting sarcasm, with never a word of praise from the old ward sisters. Medical students suffered similar treatment, but they were in the wards for a short time only each day. A small word of encouragement or an occasional smile would have worked wonders and have meant so much to us. I determined then, that if ever I attained the lofty height of Matron, or even a blue belt, I would give praise unstintingly when due.

'Many of the wards at Barts were given over to the care of the wounded. It was always a joy to work in one of these wards amongst the type of patient I knew best, but I loved the woman patients equally well, they were so brave and bore pain with such fortitude, the children, too were most lovable if somewhat exacting.

'We were prepared to do our utmost to relieve the lot of these brave men. Some of us were given responsible tasks which made me shudder to think of in later years, but "where ignorance is bliss, tis folly to be wise" and we cheerfully shouldered all the responsibility entrusted to us, and somehow, under a Divine Providence, we appeared to do little damage.

'As a probationer on night duty I developed a genius for making omelettes. Very often another night staff nurse would borrow me ten minutes in order to cook her supper, we often had an egg given us for this purpose. On one memorable occasion the phone rang in my ward about midnight, and I was summoned to the august presence of the Night Super and her assistant and ordered to apply my culinary art to the cooking of their repast. That was an honour indeed, and something to brag about for a long time.'

The City of London was no different than the rest of the country when it came to the war effort, other than there were fewer women who lived within the confines of the 'Square Mile' than most other places. Women in towns and cities all over the country undoubtedly played their part in the First World War. Not only did they have to contend with the worry that went with being a wife or mother, but they now found themselves having to take on the roles and jobs of the very men that had left them behind to go off and do their duty by fighting in the war.

Women worked either out of financial necessity, social pressure, or the specific need of government requirements. In the City of London, women worked as nurses, bus drivers, taxi drivers, secretaries as well as ticket inspectors, the demand for which was possibly greater than in most other towns and cities. Transport jobs paid five times as much as traditional female work, but women were still paid less than men. A lot has been written about how the war had changed the lives of women and provided them with economic independence, which it undoubtedly did, but the reality was that change for them had been happening for some years, and the war simply sped that process along somewhat quicker. Selfridges opening in 1909, for example, had greatly contributed massively to the feminine cause, with most of their staff being women. The suffragette movement had already been well established before the outbreak of the war.

Between 1914 and 1918 it has been estimated that more than two million women replaced men in the workplace, which opened up a much wider range of jobs to them. Before the war, one of the main roles carried out by women who worked was that of domestic servant. This changed considerably in the years after the war, but not for one particular reason. Domestic appliances, such as electric irons, cookers and vacuum cleaners, for example, curtailed the need for so many servants in many households, but this has to be looked at in the context that with the wider selection of jobs that were then available to women, working conditions were better, as were the wages paid, so all of a sudden, being a domestic servant wasn't so appealing as it had been previously.

The war had made many women widows, which then left them basically with two options. Either find another man and re-marry or go out to work in an occupation that paid a decent wage. With the war came regulations for employers concerning equal pay for both men and women who had or were doing the same work. It wasn't long however before ruthless and unscrupulous employers found lawful ways around having to pay women the same money to do the job that a man had been doing before the war.

The war years were undoubtedly difficult times for women. They had to contend with the worry of their husband, or son off fighting in the war whilst having to hold down a job, look after the home, and for some who were mothers, also having to look after their children. Some women had jobs purely for the duration of the war. Others who wanted a life in the medical field found hospitals who were more than happy to take them on as students during the war but after the war was over and the men were back home, the same desire to employ women in such roles was no longer present. It was the same in other professions as well.

With the war coming to an end in November 1918 and a General Election due just over a month later, the Government faced somewhat of a dilemma. Firstly, by 1918 there were over one million working women who were members of a union, which meant they had to be taken seriously in a political sense; and secondly, as the law stood, only men who had been resident in the country for the previous twelve months were eligible to vote. With hundreds of thousands of men having been abroad in different theatres of war that was an awful lot of men who found themselves unable to vote and with a comparatively low turnout of only 57.2%, it did not look good for the Government of the day. In the 1918 General Election 8.5 million women were eligible to vote, but that figure only represented 40% of women in the country.

A 'snapshot' of some 300 women who were living in the City of London in the years immediately leading up to the start of the war, showed that sixty-seven of them were married. There were thirty-three daughters or other female relatives who worked in such roles as clerks, dress makers, typists, milliner's, short hand typists, sales women, assistants, and one who was a coffee house worker. There were two women who had the slightly unusual jobs of being a blouse examiner and an envelope folder. Ninety women were in domestic service of some kind or another. Forty-three were patients at St Bartholomew's hospital, nearly all of whom would have lived in the immediate area. There were ten women who were widows or heads of families as well as thirteen who were either boarders or who lived at the place where they worked, such as public houses or hotels. Four of these were in fact barmaids and another two were manageresses of the pubs. They lived and worked as FANY's

The Princess Royal's Volunteer Corps, or First Aid Nursing Yeomanry (FANY's), as they are also known, were first formed in 1907 and are still in existence to this very day, making them the longest continuous uniformed voluntary military service in the world, as well as the only all-women's military unit in the United Kingdom. The Corps was actually founded by a man, Edward Baker, who was wounded at the Battle of Omdurman, near Khartoum in Sudan, on 2 September 1898, when he was a Warrant Officer in the 21st Lancers. The FANY's website recalls Baker's thoughts as he lay wounded and vulnerable on the battlefield.

'Lying there wounded nursing his left shinbone, where he'd been shot, he thought that it would be wonderful if a group of women were able to administer first aid on the battlefield to the men before they were removed to the Casualty Clearing Stations.'

It would be another nine years before Baker's dream actually became a reality.

The short extract below is taken from one of the early editions of *Women at War Gazette*, the FANY's official newspaper, in October 1910.

'On my return from active service I thought out a plan which I anticipated would meet the want, but it was not until September 1907 that I was able to found a troop of young women to see how my ideas on the subject would work. My idea was that each member of this Corps would receive, in addition to a thorough training in First Aid, a drilling in cavalry movements, signalling and camp work, so that nurses could ride onto the battlefield to attend to the wounded who might otherwise have been left to a slow death. Captain Edward Baker 1910.'

That same year, 1910, saw some disaffection within the organisation and some of the women led by Mabel St Clair Stobart, broke away and formed what became the Women's Sick and Wounded Convoy, who in 1912 went out to Serbia during the 1st Balkan war.

The First Aid Nursing Yeomanry Corps had their Headquarters in the City of London at 118 Holburn, London E.C. and their phone number was Holburn 2899. From their very early days recruits were sought who could already ride and who preferably owned their own horse, hence the word Yeomanry in the Corps title.

When looking at what a woman would have to do to become a FANY nurse, it was clear that they had to be outstanding individuals. To begin with, not only were the recruits not paid a wage, they had to pay a 10/- enrolment fee. On top of that they had to pay a 6/- monthly subscription, which suggests that those who joined would have come from some of the more affluent families of society, as not too many ordinary women would have been able to work for no wages whilst also having to pay each month for the privilege of undertaking the role.

They had to be between the ages of 17 and 35, although there was the allowance at the discretion of the Commanding officer to be outside of that age range. They had to be a minimum of 5 feet 3 inches tall, although unlike other nursing units there was no restriction on women having to be single. Once having passed those criteria, prospective recruits then had to qualify in first aid, home nursing, horse riding, veterinary work, signalling and camp cooking. The next stage after having qualified in all of these disciplines was to purchase their own uniform. If they didn't own a horse they had to pay out of their own pocket for the hire of one. They had to agree to enlist for a minimum of 12 months and determine if they wished to be considered for only home service of if they were happy to serve abroad in one of the theatres of war. Ironically it was the Belgians and French who first agreed to work with them, all of the British Regiments they had approached having refused their assistance.

At the outbreak of the war Grace Ashley Smith, who by now was in charge of the FANY, was on a ship en route to South Africa to visit her sister. During the journey she met Louis Franck, the Belgian Minister for the Colonies and she convinced him that she and her nurses could be of assistance; and by 10 September 1914 they were working at the l'Hôpital de Boulevard Leopold in Antwerp. With Germany's continuing advance across Belgium gaining pace with every passing day, Ashley-Smith and her fellow nurses just about managed to escape from Antwerp before it fell into enemy hands and make their way to Calais, before getting on board a ship to England.

Not to be deterred, on 29 October 1914 Grace Ashleigh-Smith and her team of intrepid nurses arrived in France with a motorised ambulance. Their first place of work was in a run down and dilapidated building, which before the war had been a convent school in the centre of Paris. For them it became Lamarack Hospital, where they would tend to their first patients of the war with the sound of shellfire echoing in their ears.

The FANY's website also recalls, how, in early gas attacks they would douse their sanitary towels in eau de cologne and hold them over their faces and those of the soldiers, because the men didn't have respirators in the early stages of the war. It wasn't until 1 January 1916 that the British War Office finally requested their assistance and had them replace men from the British Red Cross Society.

By the end of the war FANYs had been awarded seventeen Military Medals, twenty-seven Croix de Guerre (France), one Legion d'Honneur and had been Mentioned in Despatches on eleven occasions. One of their number, Nurse Evelyn Fidgeon Shaw received the Croix de Guerre with Palm; she first enlisted at the Corps Headquarters in Holburn, and was the only FANY killed during the war on 24 August 1918 and is buried at the Sezanne Communal Cemetery, in the Marne region of France.

There had been one man who had actually been a FANY ambulance driver, W G R Smith, who left the Corps when he received a commission into the King's Own Yorkshire Infantry as a lieutenant.

CHAPTER 8

Tower of London and Executions of German Spies

The Tower of London has stood proudly on the banks of the river Thames for centuries, looking out over the vastness of the capital, growing in size and importance alongside the city it was once there to protect. During the war it was used as a castle, a barracks, a recruitment centre, a prison, a munitions store, a military hospital and a place where those who had been convicted of spying were executed. In more recent times it has become one of the capital's leading tourist attractions.

The *Birmingham Gazette* Friday 31 July 1914 reported;

'A sudden movement of troops in London took place yesterday. At breakfast time the men of the 1st Battalion Grenadier Guards at the Tower were unexpectedly paraded, and at 10 o'clock a "double company" at "war strength" (which means 150 with reserves) were marched to Kings Cross and en-trained for Newcastle-upon-Tyne. Simultaneously, fifty men of the 3rd Battalion of the Grenadier Guards were marched from Wellington Barracks to fill the vacancies at the Tower, and 100 more marched to the Tower last night.'

Tower of London – Indoor Rifle Range.

There was no explanation for the sudden movement of the British troops, just four days before Britain's declaration of war with Germany.

The following letter was quoted in the *Dundee Courier* of Tuesday 1 December 1914

'In the service of the Fatherland
Spy Lody's letter to his friends

'The Koelnische Zeitung today publishes a letter written by Hans Lody, the German spy, who was shot at the Tower of London, to his relations at Stuttgart on the day before he was shot.

'The letter which is dated from the Tower of London, November 5, contains the following passages;

"My Dear One,

"I have trusted in God and he has decided my hour has come, and I must start on the journey through the dark valley, like so many of my comrades in this terrible war of nations. May my life be honoured as a humble offering on the altar of the Fatherland. A hero's death on the battlefield is certainly finer, but such is not to be my lot, and I die here in the enemy's country, silent and unknown, but the consciousness that I die in the service of the Fatherland makes death easy.

"The Supreme Court-Martial of London has sentenced me to death for military conspiracy. Tomorrow I shall be shot here in the Tower. It is consolation to me that I am not treated as a spy. I have had just judges, and I shall die as an officer, not as a spy.

"Farewell. God bless you.

"Hans.

"1918"'

Later in the war, the *Dundee Courier* of Tuesday 11 June 1918 had more to report on spies and the Tower of London.

The man in the Tower of London
His identity revealed in the Commons

'Mr Ronald McNeil asked if any further information could be given in respect to the prisoner in the Tower of London who was put ashore from a German submarine on the West Coast of Ireland?

Mr Macpherson replied that the man had been identified as No. 8043 Lance Corporal J Dowling, of the Connaught Rangers. He had been remanded for trial by Court-Martial under Section 45 Army Act, which dealt with offences of voluntarily aiding and serving the enemy.

Mr McNeil – Was this a deserter from the British Army? How did he get in to a German submarine?

Mr Macpherson – I do not think he can properly be called a deserter from the British Army. He was I think, a prisoner of war.

Mr King – Will the Court-Martial be public or the proceedings reported fully and fairly?

Mr Macpherson – I can quite imagine a good deal of the proceedings will not be made public.'

It transpires that Joseph Patrick Dowling was a member of what had become known as the Irish Brigade, the brain child of Sir Roger Casement, who was hanged at Pentonville prison in London on 3 August 1916 for treason. Joseph Patrick Dowling's story is a very interesting one in its own right, but in essence he was a Corporal in the 2nd Battalion, Connaught Rangers when he was involved in heavy fighting at Mons in Belgium and separated from his Regiment. He then became attached to the 306th French Regiment and was captured and taken prisoner on 3 September 1914 and eventually ended up as a prisoner of war at a camp at Limburg An Der Lahn. He remained a prisoner of war until he was released on 12 April 1918 when a German submarine surfaced off the coast of County Clare and dropped him off in a rubber dingy. He eventually landed on nearby Crab Island where he spent the night before being picked up by a local fishing boat who dropped him off at Doolin Point on the main land. When interviewed by the Coastguard he claimed that he was an American sailor by the name of James O'Brien who had been a crew member on the Mississippi which had been torpedoed by a German submarine and sunk. He was told he would have to make his way to Galway to see the senior naval officer. This meant catching a train from nearby Ennistymon. On arriving there he was detained by a policeman and the following day conveyed to Galway.

On 14 April 1918 he was taken to London and interviewed by the authorities where he gave up his true identity and admitted that he had been dropped off by a German Submarine. After being interviewed by senior members of British Naval Intelligence he was conveyed to the Tower of London on 22 April 1918. His trial by Court-Martiall took place over the 8 and 9 July 1918. He faced three charges, that whilst he was a prisoner of war in Germany he joined a hostile force, namely the Irish Brigade. That he endeavoured to induce others to join this hostile force and that he participated in an attempt to land a hostile force in Ireland. He was found guilty of all charges against him and sentenced to death by firing squad, although this was commuted to penal servitude for life.

The website of MI5 reveals that the German Archives show that they sent at least 120 spies to Britain during the course of the First World War. Only sixty-five of them were ever caught and dealt with by the British authorities, which of course begs the question whatever happened to the other fifty-five and how much 'useful' information did they manage to obtain and send back to their spy masters in Germany who worked for the German Naval Intelligence service. The other question of course is, if sixty-five spies were caught by MI5 and only

The Tower of London 1915.

twelve of them were executed, what became of the other fifty-three?

It is noticeable that no German spies were executed after April 1916, even though the number of MI5's staff gradually increased throughout the war, finally reaching a total of 844. The reduction in executions of German spies after April 1916 is not necessarily an indication that there were not any operating throughout Great Britain after this time, but more because throughout the second half of the war MI5's attention was directed towards counter-subversion in the mis-belief that the growing number of British industrial disputes were being inflamed by direct Communist interference.

There were twelve spies shot at the Tower of London during the First World War. They were the first people to be executed there for one hundred and seventy years.

Carl Hans Lody was a lieutenant in the German Naval Reserve and already in military service before the outbreak of the war, volunteering for the Naval Intelligence Department in May 1914. He was executed for being a German spy on 6 November 1914, at the Tower of London by members of the 3rd Battalion, Grenadier Guards. His trial took place at The Middlesex Guildhall, Westminster on Friday, Saturday and Monday 30, 31 October and 1 November 1914. He was charged with two offences under the Defence of the Realm Act 1914.

Carl Hans Lody.

- Attempting to convey information calculated to be useful to an enemy by sending a letter from Edinburgh on 27 September 1914 to Herr J. Stammer in Berlin, which contained information with regard to the defences and preparations for war of Great Britain.
- Committed war treason against Great Britain by sending a letter from Dublin, around 30 September 1914, to Herr J. Stammer in Berlin which contained information with regard to the defence and preparations for war of Great Britain.

As Lody was a member of the German Navy the trial was held before a Military Courts-Martial. The Judge Advocate was Mr Kenneth Marshal, Barrister at Law with Carl Lody, being defended by Mr George Elliot, KC, Mr Roland Harker and Messers Hewitt, Urquart and Woolacot. Lody pleaded not guilty to both charges.

When Lody was arrested at Killarney, the Police found the details of two telegrams which he had sent as well as some German gold amongst the items he had in his possession. Unbeknown to him the letters and telegrams which he had sent had been intercepted by the British and examined for their content in London.

He was found guilty of both charges. After his execution was carried out his body was initially buried in the grounds of the Tower of London before eventually being re-buried in the East London Cemetery in Plaistow, London. John Fraser, who was a Yeoman Warder at the Tower of London at the time, wrote an account of Lody's execution.

'The following morning, 6 November 1914, broke cold, foggy and bleak, and at a very early hour Lody was brought from his cell (29 Casements), and the grim procession formed up on the verandah of the Tower Main Guard. It was led by the Chaplain, solemnly reading the Burial Service, followed by the prisoner, with an armed escort marching on either side of him, and the

Edinburgh, Sept 4th 14.

Mr. A. Burchard.
                    Stockholm

Dear Sir –

Will you kindly communicate with
Berlin at once by wire (code or whatever
system at your disposal) and inform them
that on Sept 3d great masses of Russian
soldiers have passed through Edinburgh
on their way to London and France –
Although it must be expected that Berlin
has knowledge of these movements, which
probably took its start at Archangle –
it may be well to forward this information. It is estimated here, that
60000 men has passed, a number
which seem greatly exaggerated. I
went to the depot (station) and
noticed trains passing through at
high speed, blinds down. The landing
in Scotland took place at Aberdeen.
                    Yours very truly
                              Charles

Letter from Carl Hans Lody to his handler in Stockholm.

Carl Hans Lody envelope.

firing party of eight stalwart guardsman bringing up the rear.

'Nobody liked this sort of thing. It was altogether too coldblooded for an ordinary stomach (particularly that of a soldier, who hates cold bloodiness) to face with equanimity, and it is not too much to say that, of that sad little procession, the calmest and most composed member was the condemned man himself.

'For the Chaplain, in particular, it was a bad time. He had never had a similar experience, and his voice had a shake in it as he intoned the solemn words of the Burial Service over the living form of the man it most concerned. His hands, too as he held the book, trembled a little, the more honour to him!

'The escort and the firing-party, too, were far from comfortable, and one could see that the slow march suitable to the occasion was getting badly on their nerves. They wanted to hurry over it and get the beastly business finished.

'But the prisoner walked steadily, stiffly upright, and yet as easily unconcerned as though he was going to a tea party, instead to his death. His eyes were upturned to the gloomy skies, and his nostrils eagerly drank in the precious air that was soon to be denied them. But his face was quite calm and composed, almost expressionless.

'Then came a queer and pathetic little incident. As they came to the end of the verandah, the Chaplain, in his nervousness, made to turn left, which was the wrong way. Instantly Lody took a quick step forward, caught the Chaplain by the right arm, and with a polite and kindly smile, gently guided him to the right, the correct way.

'A few moments later the procession disappeared through the doorway of the sinister shed, and shortly after that came the muffled sound of a single volley. Carl Lody had paid!

When I think of Carl Lody a phrase always slips in to my head, just three little words: "A gentleman, unafraid!"'

Although Lody appears not to have been a particularly effective spy, he was certainly well thought of and respected.

An article in the *Derby Daily Telegraph* on Wednesday 11 November 1914, reported that Lody's execution took place in the Tower's miniature rifle range just as dawn was breaking. He refused the offer of a blindfold, calmly sat down on a chair at the far end of the range, folded his arms, crossed his legs and leant back awaiting his inevitable fate.

In 1935 a memorial in the shape of a statue of a knight in full armour was unveiled in his home town of Lubeck in Germany. The knight's hands are fettered, and a serpent, symbolising betrayal, twines round his feet. In January 1937 a new German destroyer was named after Carl Lody and in February 1937 a play about him opened in Berlin and was performed to audiences throughout the country to mark Germany's Heroes Remembrance Day. The play emphasised how Lody was treated by the British throughout his trial and the manner in which he met his death.

Karl Frederick Muller was born in Libau in Latvia in 1857 and by 1899 he was married and living in Antwerp in Belgium. An intelligent man who was fluent in several languages including English and German. It is believed that whilst living in Antwerp he was recruited by the German Secret Service in December 1915.

He arrived in England at Hull on 11 January 1915 having sailed from Rotterdam two days earlier. On his arrival he went to stay with friends of his who lived in Sunderland. Two days later he had arrived in London. How or why he came to the attention of the British authorities in the first place is not clear, but they intercepted letters he had written in English only to discover that they also contained sentences in German which had been written in invisible ink.

Whilst staying in London he had met a man by the name of John Hahn who he had previously known in Antwerp. Although born in England both of Hahn's parents were in fact German. Both men were arrested in London, Hahn on 24 February 1915 and Muller the following day. The trial against both men took place between 2 and 4 June 1915 at the Central Criminal Courts of the Old Bailey. Hahn pleaded guilty and was sentenced to seven years Penal Servitude, whilst Muller pleaded not guilty. Despite his protestations Muller was found guilty and sentenced to death by firing squad. Not surprisingly with nothing to lose and everything to gain, he appealed against his conviction which was turned down on 21 June 1915. Two days later he was executed at the Tower of London. Muller had been held at Brixton Prison since his arrest and subsequent trial and only brought to the Tower of London the day before his execution. He went to his death at 0600 hours on 23 June 1915; he was fifty-seven years of age.

Karl Frederick Muller.

Sir Basil Thomson, who at the time was the Assistant Commissioner of the Metropolitan Police later wrote the following account of Muller's execution.

'On Wednesday 23 June at 6am, in the miniature Rifle Range at the Tower, the prisoner was calm, shook hands with me and thanked me. I led him to the chair which was tied to short stakes driven into the ground, he sat on it quietly and the Sergeant buckled a leather strap round his body and the back of the chair and then blindfolded him with a cloth. The firing party consisted of 8 guardsmen. I watched as closely as possible and went to him immediately after he was shot. I saw no expression of pain. I found no pulse and no sign of life. Death appeared to be instantaneous, and the body retained the same position. The bullets probably in fragments had passed through the thorax and out the back. Some blood, mixed with what appeared to be bone, had escaped through the clothing and 7 or 8 drops had fallen to the ground. The body was carried on a stretcher into the isolation ward.'

Willem Johannes Roos and Haicke Marinus Petrius Janssen were both executed at the Tower of London in the early hours of 30 July 1915, having been found guilty of spying for Germany. Janssen was the first to be shot followed ten minutes later by Roos.

Janssen arrived at Hull by ship from Holland on 12 May 1915, his passport showing that he was Dutch and that his occupation was that of a cigar salesman. Having spent just over a week in the North East, Janssen travelled down to London before continuing on to Southampton where he arrived on 22 May 1915. Whilst there he sent and received several telegrams to and from Dirks & Co, the cigar company he worked for in the Hague, all of which were intercepted by the British authorities. He was arrested in Southampton on 30 May 1915 and subsequently taken to London for interrogation.

Haicke Marinus Petrius Janssen

Roos had arrived in Britain the day after Janssen, on 13 May 1915, starting off in London before he travelled on to Newcastle and ended up in Edinburgh. He too had used the story that he was a cigar salesman from Holland working for Dierks & Co in The Hague, to where he had also sent telegrams and a postcard.

Willem Johannes Roos.

Both Janssen and Roos had been sending coded messages back to Germany about the movement and location of British naval ships. Roos was arrested in Edinburgh on 2 June 1915 and also taken back to London for interrogation. Both men were charged with spying for Germany and placed before a Courts Martial, both of which took place at the Middlesex Guildhall, Westminster,

London. Janssen was tried first on 16 July 1915 and offered no defence or made no statement. Not surprisingly he was found guilty and sentenced to death by firing squad.

Roos's trial took place the very next day and he too was found guilty of spying for Germany; he was also sentenced to death by firing squad. Both men were executed at the Tower of London in the early hours of 30 July 1915, by soldiers from the Scots Guards, ten minutes apart. Both men were described in reports of the day as being brave as they met their fate, Roos even refusing a blindfold, although what must have gone through his mind as he approached the chair he was to be shot in seeing it splattered with Janssen's still warm blood, can only be guessed.

Ernst Waldemar Melin.

Ernst Waldemar Melin was Swedish by birth but at the outbreak of the war he was working in the Russian town of Nikolaieff. He lost his job and made his way to Hamburg in Germany which is where it would appear that that he agreed to become a spy for the Germans. He arrived in London on 12 January 1915 and found lodgings in Hampstead nearby to Belsize Park Underground station.

After members of the British Security Services intercepted mail that was intended for Melin, it became absolutely clear that he was spying for the Germans; before this they had only suspected he was, but now they had actual evidence against him to prove it. He was arrested by police officers late in the evening on 14 June 1915 at his lodgings in Hampstead. His Court Martial took place over 20 and 21 June 1915 at the Middlesex Guildhall and once again, part of the prosecution team was Mr Bodkin. Melin was found guilty of spying for German Intelligence and sentenced to death by firing squad. He was executed at the Tower of London at 0600 hours on 10 September 1915 by soldiers from the Scots Guards in the Towers miniature rifle range. He was forty-nine years of age.

On 30 May 1915 Augusto Alfredo Roggen, a Uruguayan who was born in Montivideo in 1881, arrived at Tilbury docks on board the SS

Batavia, which had sailed from Rotterdam in Holland. He then made his way up to Edinburgh under the pretence of being a farmer, arriving there on 5 June where he booked in to the Carlton hotel. Whilst in the capital he did some sight seeing, went on a daytrip to the nearby Trossachs and registered with the local police, which was a wartime requirement for foreign nationals visiting and travelling round Great Britain.

Augusto Alfredo Roggen.

Whilst in Edinburgh he did what most tourists would do and sent a couple of postcards. There were addressed to somebody by the name of H. Flores at an address in Rotterdam, Holland. Unfortunately for Roggen, the address he had sent the postcards to was well known to the British Security Services, which not surprisingly then brought him to their close attention. The details on the postcards were copied before they were forwarded on to the address in Holland. At the time the German Consul in Rotterdam played an active part in in all of their country's intelligence operations, so it is inconceivable to think that Roggen was not working for them. He arrived at the Tarbet Hotel, Loch Lomond, on 9 June and within only five hours of being at the hotel he was arrested during a police raid on his room, during which they found a loaded Browning revolver, with fifty rounds of ammunition, some invisible ink, (believed to be Argyrol) and a map of the area which included Loch Long and a list of contacts. His real reason for travelling to Great Britain was to observe and if possible, photograph the work that was going on at Loch Long at the Arrochar Torpedo range which had been opened in 1912.

He was taken to London by Superintendent John Wright where on arrival he was handed over to Dectective Inspector Edmund Buckley from the Metropolitan Police's Special Branch department. When interviewed he offered no defence to the allegations of spying that had been made against him. At his subsequent trial at the Middlesex Guildhall in Westminster, on 20 August he was found guilty and sentenced to death by firing squad. The sentence was carried out at the Tower of London at 0600 hours on 17 September 1915, by members of the 3rd Battalion of the Scots Guards. He was thirty-four years of age.

Luckily for the British authorities but unluckily for him, he was not that good a spy and his purpose for being in Scotland was all too easily ascertained. Once sentenced to death by the British authorities, it was the Uruguayan and not the German government, who made a request for clemency for Roggen, even though he was undoubtedly working and spying for Germany when he was captured.

Fernando Buschman.

Although he was born in Paris in 1890, Fernando Buschman's parents were Danish by birth but had become naturalised Brazilians. When he was a boy his parents had sent him to be educated in Vienna, Austria. In his adult life Buschman was a business man who had tried and failed to make his fortune in different adventures which ranged from the import and export of food stuffs to trying to manufacture airplanes.

He first arrived in London on 14 April 1915, initially staying at the Piccadilly Hotel then moving on to the Strand Palace Hotel, before moving in to lodgings in Harrington Road, South Kensington. During his time in London, he was in contact with Dierks & Co in Holland, by telegram; they had even sent money transfers to him. This was the same business that previous German spies Roos and Janssen had claimed to be cigar salesmen for, and whom the British Secret Services knew was a front for German espionage.

It is amazing to think that German Intelligence didn't know that the British Secret Service had already rumbled Dierks. It was something which would directly lead to the execution of more of their spies. As soon as somebody in England contacted them or Dierks returned the contact, those individuals immediately became persons of interest to the British Intelligence Service. It would appear this was certainly the case with Buschman and he was arrested at his lodgings in South Kensington on 5 June 1915 by Inspector George Riley who was stationed at New Scotland Yard.

Fernando Buschman was placed before a court martial, which was once again held at the Middlesex Guildhall on 29 & 30 September. He pleaded not guilty to the charges of being a German spy, but to no avail. He was found guilty and sentenced to death by firing squad. The sentence was carried out at 0700 hours on 19 October by soldiers from the 3rd Battalion, Scots Guards in the miniature rifle range at the Tower of London. Buschman's last wish was to be allowed to play his violin the night before his execution. The request was granted.

Georg Traugott Breeckow was born in Stettin (Also spelt Szezcin) in 1882 which at the time was in Germany, but today it is the capital city of the West Pomeranian Voivodesip in Poland. When he was a young man he travelled to America and became a United States' citizen, where he worked in the piano industry. He returned to Germany on 28 May 1914. He went to work for the Bureau of Foreign

Georg Traugott Breeckow.

Affairs. He was issued with a new passport in the name of Reginald Rowland and was told that he would be going to England but would be stopping off at The Hague on the way to meet a Mr Dierks. Hilmar Dierks was a spymaster and his company was a front.

Breeckow finally arrived in England on 11 May 1915 at Gravesend. From there he made his way to London where he booked in to the Ivanhoe Hotel, Bloomsbury Street. His contact in London was a Mrs Wertheim who had already been recruited by German Intelligence. After they met they travelled to Bournemouth together where they booked into the Grand Hotel; after staying there for a few days they travelled around to other locations, most of which were naval towns. Beeckow and Wertheim returned to London on 3 June, Beeckow staying at the Imperial Hotel and Wertheim to lodgings at 62 Hammersmith Road.

He then sent a letter to H Flores at 127a Binneweg in Rotterdam, the same person and address he had sent a letter to when he was in Bournemouth. Both the name and address were already known to the British Security Service who had intercepted Breeckow's letters. On 4 June, he was arrested at the Imperial Hotel by Metropolitan Police detectives. Whilst searching his room the Police discovered some rice paper inside a shaving brush. The paper contained the names of several Royal Navy ships, written in Breeckow's hand writing. Wertheim was arrested at her lodgings five days later on 9 June.

They were tried together at the Central Criminal Courts of the Old Bailey between 14 and 17 September, where both of them pleaded not guilty to the charges of spying for Germany. They were both found guilty, Wertheim was given a ten year prison sentence which she initially served at Aylesbury Prison, but in 1918 and with failing health, she was sent to what was then known as the Broadmoor Criminal Lunatic Asylum, where she died on 29 July 1920 of pulmonary tuberculosis. Breeckow was sentenced to death by firing squad. He was executed by soldiers from the 3rd Battalion, Scots Guards, strapped to a wooden chair at the miniature rifle range at the Tower of London on 26 October 1915. He was thirty-three years of age.

Unlike previous spies who had been executed at the Tower, history records that Breeckow wasn't calm and composed, quite the opposite in fact. When it came time for him to make his way from his cell on that fateful morning, he was in a state of near collapse and became quite agitated. Even though he was strapped to a wooden chair he was described as 'shivering with fright.' Amazingly the subsequent inquest showed that Breeckow had actually died of heart failure before the soldiers shots had impacted on his body, although his death certificate stated that he died of 'violent gunshot wounds of the chest.'

Irving Guy Ries was an American, born in Chicago in 1860. It is believed his real name could possibly have been Carl Paul Julius Hensel, as he never revealed his true identity, possibly out of not wanting to bring shame on his family. He arrived in England on 4 July 1915 at Liverpool, having sailed from New York, purporting to be a sales representative for two American firms in the corn and hay industry. He then took a train to London where he booked a room at the Hotel Cecil in the Strand. He came to the attention of the British Security Services within a matter of days when a telegram, transferring the rather large sum of £40, arrived for him from an address in Holland, an address which was already known to the British authorities.

Irving Guy Ries.

On 15 July, Ries travelled to Liverpool, then on to Newcastle, followed by Glasgow, Edinburgh, back to Liverpool before arriving back in London at the Hotel Cecil, on 28 July. He made a catastrophic decision on 9 August 1915 when he decided upon a visit to the American Embassy in London. He had to go to Rotterdam in Holland and needed a visa. When his passport was examined by the embassy official who was dealing with him it was discovered to be a forgery. Ries was allowed to leave but the embassy immediately contacted the police. The very next day Ries was arrested at the Hotel Cecil.

He was tried by a court martial, which was once again held at the Middlesex Guildhall over two days on 28 and 29 September and despite his protestations that he was innocent of any crime, he was found guilty and sentenced to death by firing squad. Ries's trial, or more his conviction, was somewhat unusual as unlike previous spies who had been executed, he had not been caught conveying any information to his contacts in Germany. After his trial and subsequent conviction he had been held at Wandsworth prison, only being taken to the Tower of London the day before his execution. Before sitting on the chair that would soon support his lifeless body, he requested that he might be allowed the opportunity to shake hands with the very men who were to take his life and send him to meet his maker. He then walked up the line of soldiers who were about to take his life, greeting each of them politely as he went saying, 'You are only doing your duty as I have done mine.' To be that calm at such a time, considering the situation he was in, whilst at the same time remaining polite and courteous to the very men who were just about to take his life, showed remarkable strength and depth of character.

Ries was executed at 0700 hours on 27 October, the day after Georg Traugott Breeckow met the same fate. He was fifty-five years of age.

Albert Meyer was twenty-two years of age and claimed to be Dutch although this was never conclusively confirmed. It was more likely that he was either German or Turkish. He was well travelled, having lived and worked in Germany, Spain and Italy before the war. In June 1914 he was working in Oxford Street in London. In March the following year he travelled to Copenhagen via Holland and Germany before returning back to the UK two months later, moving in to lodgings in Soho, London. On 20 May, Meyer married Catherine

Rebecca Godleman at St. Pancras Registry Office in London.

The British Security Services had intercepted a couple of letters sent to an address that was known to them in The Hague, Holland, which were eventually traced back to Meyer. He was arrested and tried by a court martial at the Middlesex Guildhall on 5 and 6 November. He was found guilty of being a German spy and sentenced to death by firing squad. He decided on appealing the verdict as was his legal right, but his appeal failed. He was shot at the Tower of London at 0745 hours on 2 December 1915, by soldiers from the 3rd Battalion, Scots Guards. His execution wasn't like any of the previous executions.

Albert Meyer.

He became hysterical, started shouting at his captors and began struggling with his guards. Even after having being strapped into the chair Meyer was screaming at those who were about to end his life, silence only prevailing as the bullets tore into body.

Ludovico Hurwitz-y-Zender holds the distinction of being the last person to be executed at the Tower of London during the First World War. He was born in Lima, Peru in 1878 and was a well-educated individual, who could speak both English and French fluently. He left Peru just after the war broke out and made his way to England stating that he was a salesman looking to trade in handkerchiefs, paper and different food products. In May 1915, British Security Services had intercepted

Ludovico Hurwitz-y-Zender.

telegrams sent by Zender to an address they knew was connected to German Intelligence in Oslo. Each of the telegrams were signed in his name and included an address of 59 Union Street, Glasgow.

Police decided to act immediately and sent officers to arrest him, but Zender had, by sheer coincidence, already left for Bergen via Newcastle. Zender arrived back at Newcastle on board the SS *Vega* on 2 July 1915, he was immediately arrested and taken to London to be interrogated. Zender's cover story was that he was ordering sardines and other tinned fish for export back to Peru. The British Security Services managed to work out that in the telegrams he had been sending to his contact in Oslo, the references to shipments of tinned fish were in fact shipping movements from different ports along the coastline of the Firth of Forth.

His court martial took place between 20 and 22 March 1916 at Caxton Hall, Westminster, London. He pleaded not guilty to the charges against him, but all to no avail. He was found guilty and sentenced to death by firing squad. Zender appealed the Courts decision which was upheld. He was executed at the Tower of London at 0700 hours on 11 April 1916. He was thirty-eight years of age. The distinction of being executed before a firing squad rather than being hanged would appear to be because they were captured and treated as enemy combatants, regardless of whether they were actually military personnel in its truest sense. Ultimately they were employed by the German Intelligence Service, which meant they were viewed as being military personnel rather than civilians.

Robert Rosenthal was hanged at Wandsworth Prison in London for spying under the Treachery Act 1914, on 15 July 1915. He had reported shipping movements of British vessels to the German Navy. Coincidentally, after his initial arrest on 5 July 1915, Rosenthal was held in the Guardroom at the Tower of London before later being transferred to Wandsworth Barracks and then on to Wandsworth prison where he was hanged.

Sir Roger David Casement was born in Dublin on 1 September 1864. He went on to become an Irish Nationalist, activist and poet. He became famous for the reporting of human rights abuses in the Congo and Peru. In August 1914, he travelled with John Devoy to New York in America, to meet with German diplomat, Count Bernstorff and put a proposition to him that if Germany would sell guns to the Irish and provide them with military leaders they would stage a revolt against

England, and in doing so divert troops from the war on the Western Front. Although the plan was received positively, it was never actually implemented. In November 1914 Casement negotiated a declaration of intent from Germany, it said;

> 'The Imperial Government formally declares that under no circumstances would Germany invade Ireland with a view to its conquest or the overthrow of any native institutions in that country. Should the fortune of this Great War, that was not of Germany's seeking, ever bring in its course German troops to the shores of Ireland, they would land there not as an Army of invaders to pillage and destroy but as the forces of a Government that is inspired by goodwill towards a country and a people for whom Germany desires only national prosperity and national freedom.'

Casement also tried to recruit an Irish Brigade which consisted of Irish prisoners of war held by Germany in the camp at Limburg an der Lahn who would be mobilized to fight against the English. Germany wasn't totally convinced by either Casement or his proposals although they did see the benefits to their own cause of an Irish uprising against the British. They offered the Irish 20,000 rifles that were twenty-five years old, ten machine-guns with ammunition for all of the weapons, which wasn't anywhere near the numbers Casement had been hoping for. In the end the weapons never arrived in Ireland. The British Security Service discovered their imminent arrival and intercepted them before they could be delivered to their intended destination. Before the Easter Rising in Ireland in 1916, Casement had sought German support for a rebellion in Ireland against British rule. When he arrived back in Ireland he was arrested for treason, tried and found guilty. He was hanged at Pentonville Prison in London on 3 August 1916.

CHAPTER 9

City of London Police

Although there had been a form of policing within the City since as far back as Roman times, the City of London Police was formed in 1839 as a direct result of the City of London Police Act of that year, when a body of 500 men were sworn in as constables.

The Commissioner of the Force throughout the First World War years, was Sir William Nott-Bower. It was a position he held for twenty-three years, beginning in 1902 and not retiring until 1925 when he was seventy-six years of age. He was knighted in 1911. He was a man with a

The City of London Police Crest.

military past having served in both the King's Regiment and as a captain in the 5th (Militia) Battalion, West Yorkshire Regiment, before he started out on his police career with the Royal Irish Constabulary. He became the Chief Constable of Leeds Constabulary and the Head Constable of the Liverpool Constabulary in October 1881.

At the outset of the First World War the City of London Police were fortunate enough to possess two electrically powered ambulances. They acquired a third during the war in 1915, which they still had two years after Sir William had retired, in 1927. Although the square mile was fortunate enough not to have suffered too badly as a result of Zeppelin and aircraft raids during the war, their ambulances still remained invaluable. It was in 1904 when Sir William had submitted his views on acquiring ambulances for use by the force to his police committee.

To evidence his report he used the information that in the previous year his officers had needed to convey 1,705 people to hospital, which was more than 140 per month. The only way his men could do this was to strap the injured person to one of the force's hand wheeled litters, which was not ideal for all concerned.

It took three years before the plan came to fruition, but Sir William finally got approval for his ambulances, and did better than he could have possibly hoped for. He had been hoping to receive permission and approval from his police committee to be able to purchase horses which could be used for multi purposes, which would include pulling the ambulances, similar to what he had put in place in Liverpool. Instead he was given approval to purchase an electrically driven motor ambulance from the Electro Mobile Company in Mayfair; and so it was that on 13 May 1907 the City of London Police Ambulance Service came into being. A second ambulance would follow in 1909. The original ambulance was stationed at St Bartholomew's Hospital's Pathology block, but it was staffed by police officers, who were both the driver and assistant.

Sir William had ensured that all of his officers were first aid trained. The force even had their own hospital, which was located on the top floor of the Bishopsgate Police station and came in very useful. Officers who were either sick or had been injured on duty and were expecting to be unfit to carry out their duties for more than three days, were obliged to attend the hospital so that they could be medically examined, and if need be, admitted for further treatment, all of which was totally free of charge. The hospital was staffed by a surgeon, a matron and three nurses. Officers who had been placed on light duties due to their sickness or injuries, were sometimes required to work there as orderlies.

The possibility of war in Europe had been a present factor for a few years prior to its actual commencement in August 1914. With this in mind the Government had directed all local authorities throughout the country to ensure that they had police reserves, sufficient to deal with possible emergency situations, as far back as 1911. Sir William decided on a two pronged approach. His first option was to utilise retired police officers who would be recalled to the service and used as uniformed constables. Secondly, he would utilise civilian volunteers.

Once the war started, a large number of Sir William's full time officers left to enlist in the armed forces, meaning that he needed to start calling upon the officers in his first reserve, and the Special Constabulary, who did not wear uniform, only a red and white striped arm band. They were also provided with a wooden truncheon. The civilian volunteers, who in effect became the Reserve, were often called out, especially when there was the threat of an air raid.

The City's first experience of a German air raid came on the evening of 8 September 1915 when Zeppelins dropped incendiaries in the area of Fenchurch Street. The raids continued the following evening when a group of Zeppelins dropped a combination of incendiary and high explosive bombs over the City, which killed six people and injured a further thirty-eight. It would be nearly another two years before there were any more air raids on the City, but these new raids saw a real change in tactics. Firstly they were not carried out by Zeppelins, but rather Gotha aeroplanes, and the raids were no longer carried out under the cover of darkness, making them potentially a lot more dangerous.

On the morning of 13 June 1917, fourteen German aircraft appeared over the City, and dropped a total of seventy-two bombs in the Liverpool Street area in just two minutes. By the time the raid was over, 158 people, including children, had been killed and another 411 had been injured.

Then, on the evening of 30 August 1918, the entire City of London Police force, along with fellow officers from other Forces up and down the country, went out on strike. A lot of officers had been secretly joining the National Union of Police and Prison Officers, which had been in existence since September 1913, but anyone found to be a member of it faced instant dismissal. This was endorsed on the eve of the strike by the Government, who assumed that the threat of being sacked and the loss of pension rights, would be a sufficient deterrent, but they misread the feeling and the strike went ahead. The strikers' demands included recognition of their Union as well as better pay and conditions. During the war years the cost of living had doubled whilst police pay had stayed the same, making its value less in real terms. At the time of the strike the prime minister, David Lloyd George, was in France. He made his way back to London and met with the Executive of NUPPO the next day. All of the Unions demands were met, except the one which gave them official recognition.

By the end of the war the City of London Police had lost forty of its men whilst they were serving in the armed forces. There was a memorial service held to commemorate their loss on Sunday 22 June 1919, at St Botolph's Church in Bishopsgate, even though the war would not officially be over for another six days with the signing of the Treaty of Versailles on 28 June 1919.

PC78 B	W E Abery	PC150 B	H Mansell
PC11 D	C L Allard	PC77 A	E T Morris
PC140 B	J Brown	PC 282 C	T Minke
PC80 D	C Evans	PC186 B	J Moore
PC227 B	J E Cashmore	PC193 C	A Morgan
PC88 D	A E Cooke	PC122 A	T G S Meheux
PC174 C	W Cooper	PC105 B	H G Midmer
PC152 B	G F Coffin	PC100 B	G Matthews
PC190 B	F Cull	PC112 D	D McDonald
PC70 A	W B Drayner	PC274 B	J McDowell
PC247 C	A J Eddenden	PC91 C	E Robson
PC263 C	W Hill	PC61 A	R J Rout
PC130 C	R Hodge	PC534 A	G F Rose
PC300 D	J Imlach	PC206 D	G F Tomkins
PC133 C	H Ive	PC182 C	J Tyne
PC244 A	J Jordan	PC89 A	A J Taylor
PC154 B	G Kemp	PC92 C	H White
PC250 C	A Lister	PC 146 D	S Weeks
PC308 D	S S Ludwig	PC223 C	A R Woodrow
PC79 C	F Lebentz	PC75 E	H S White

All of the above officers had been serving in the City of London Police at the outbreak of the First World War, and left to enlist in his Majesty's Armed Forces. The first of them to be killed was Alfred John Taylor who was killed in action on 26 August 1914. He was a private in the 1st Battalion, Rifle Brigade and is buried at the La Ferye-Sous-Jouarre Memorial Cemetery in France.

The first few of months of the war was not a good time for the City of London Police. Five of them had been killed before the end of the year. Three of whom, who had all joined the Royal Navy, had all been killed by the end of the October and two of them had died on the same day.

Harry George Midmer was a 22 year old Able Seaman (SS/2026) in the Royal Navy serving on HMS *Cressy*, when he was killed in action on 22 September 1914. He has no known grave and his name is commemorated on the Chatham Naval Memorial.

The same day saw the death of William Bruce Drayner who was also an Able Seaman (205138) in the Royal Navy, serving on HMS *Hogue*. He was 30 years of age. Like Midmer, his name is commemorated on the Chatham Naval Memorial.

Thomas George Shelton Meheux, a Leading Seaman in the Royal Navy, was killed in action on 15 October 1914, whilst serving on HMS *Hawke*. He is the third member of the City of London Police, who is commemorated on the Chatham War Memorial.

CHAPTER 10

Victory and the City of London

It was December 1918, after more than four years of bloody and barbaric fighting the war was finally over. Great Britain and her allies had beaten the German Empire and her allies, but at a hefty price. Millions from both sides had died and millions more had been wounded and injured, some of whom would never properly recover. The hope now was that it wouldn't all be in vain, and that globally there would be a lasting peace. The aftermath of the war was about reconstruction and moving forward in a positive way. It was about a new beginning, like a phoenix rising from the flames of destruction. It was about businesses and organisations learning from the desolation of the war and making the prospect of a brighter tomorrow, an actual reality. Nowhere was this point high-lighted more than in the December 1918 issue of the St Bartholomew's Hospital *Journal*.

'Now we must turn to what the termination of the World War is to mean to us as a hospital and as a profession. It should mean the beginning of greater things in our history, already truly great. It is not enough for us to rest on our past; we must consider the future. A true reconstruction does not mean the destruction of our heritage, but the building up on its sure foundation of an edifice which will be of still greater service to humanity. The ideals of our profession, both the medical and the nursing, are essentially scientific and humanitarian, and unless we keep these ideals always in the foreground, our reconstruction will be but an empty sham.

'We shall have to reconstruct in our medical school, in our nursing school, in research, in medical practice, and in the new relations which are arising between our profession and the public. Let us therefore put our whole energy in to the matter, and let us make ourselves worthy of the men and women who have set us so great an example in their unparalleled devotion and sacrifice.'

Those words could just as easily sit with any business or organisation that was starting out again after the end of the First World War.

In the photograph below, notice the City of London police officer in the forefront next to the lamppost. He is wearing two medals on his

Women's Army Auxiliary Corps marching through the City of London in the Victory Parade.

Massed crowds fill the streets.

chest. Campaign medals for the First World War were not issued until 1921 at the earliest, which would mean they are either gallantry medals or campaign medals from previous conflicts such as the 2nd Boer War (1899-1902).

Although the signing of the Armistice on 11 November 1918 saw an end to the fighting, the formal peace treaty with Germany, the Treaty of Versailles, wasn't signed until 28 June 1919 as part of the Paris Peace Conference. The British Government had made plans for a public celebration to commemorate the end of the war, but were undecided on how best this could be achieved. They set up a Peace Committee which was chaired by Lord Curzon, the Foreign Secretary.

The initial idea was for a four day celebration in August of 1919, but this was eventually changed to a one day celebration which took place on Saturday 19 July. The streets along the chosen route of the Victory Parade were packed from eight o'clock in the morning. Some

London's Victory March Celebrations at Hyde Park Corner.

15,000 servicemen, and women from such organisations as the Women's Army Auxiliary Corps (WAAC) and the Voluntary Aid Detachment (VAD), took part in the parade, which culminated with a spectacular fireworks display in Hyde Park at 9.45pm.

The Cenotaph in Whitehall was unveiled on the morning of the Victory Parade, but because of the time scale between the signing of the Treaty of Versailles and the chosen date of the parade, the erection of the actual Cenotaph which was to be made from Portland stone, was not going to be possible in time. What was unveiled on the day was a replica made out of wood and plaster. It would be another year before the actual permanent structure which is in place today was erected.

The *Dundee Courier* carried the following article in its edition of Monday 21 July 1919 about the Victory March in London.

Beatty and Haig the Popular Idols
Magnificent Panorama of Empire's Strength
'Londoners on Saturday viewed a magnificent panorama of the Empire's strength in the Victory march. Nocturnal enthusiasts saw the dawn break over a flag enveloped City, with all the aspects of a fine day. At eight o'clock Hyde Park was black with people, while at the Albert Gate the small crowd which had

gathered during the night had grown to enormous dimensions. 'Marshal Foch, Sir Douglas Haig, General Pershing, Sir David Beatty, and other Allied leaders had tremendous ovations as they took their positions.

Popular Idols.

'General Pershing and the American troops had a great reception, and the enthusiasm of the crowds increased in volume as Marshal Foch approached, but it can be said that the greatest outburst of enthusiasm was reserved for Admiral Sir David Beatty and the mighty men of valour who followed him. These included mine sweepers, RNVR, and the Mercantile Marine. Admiral Beatty, a modest figure, was obviously moved by the reception accorded. Second only to the warmth of the reception given to Sir David was that given to Sir Douglas Haig and the distinguished Generals and the units of the British Army who played such an important part in the victory. The crowd was obviously moved by the presence of the remnants of the original Expeditionary Force and by the sight of the massed standards and colours surmounted by laurel wreaths.'

The king took the salute of the marching troops from his specially erected pavilion which was situated on the steps of the Victoria Memorial. Other Royal dignitaries were present as well as senior politicians, both past and those who were in office at the time.

Besides General Pershing's presence at the festivities, there were also 3,000 American soldiers, out of a total of 10,000 troops who were representing all of the other Allied nations, taking part in the march past. The general was also presented with a Sword of Honour and lunched with the king at Buckingham Palace as a guest of the Army Council. At the end of the celebrations, Sir Douglas Haig was taken ill and had to be driven home. It later transpired that he was suffering with only slight exhaustion

CHAPTER 11

Memorials and Places to Visit

In 1999, the United Kingdom National Inventory of War Memorials (UKNIWM) was set up to try and record the memorials which had been erected after the end of the First World War. It was a joint initiative between the Imperial War Museum in London and the Royal Commission on the Historic Monuments of England. So far they have managed to trace and record a staggering 5,525 memorials just for the London district alone, which includes 951 for the City of Westminster and 378 for the City of London. Some of them are discussed below.

Liverpool Street Railway Station has an amazing memorial to the more than 1,000 members of staff of the Great Eastern Railway. Above the names of those who died is the following inscription:

'To the glory of God and in grateful memory of those members of the Great Eastern Railway staff who in response to the call of their King and country sacrificed their lives during the Great War.'

There is a remarkable story which goes with this memorial. On 13 June 1917 the station was hit by three bombs which were dropped during a German daytime bombing raid of the city. Two of the bombs exploded next to a number of passenger trains, resulting in many civilian deaths. More bombs were dropped at other locations across the city which

Liverpool Street Railway Station Roll of Honour.

resulted in the deaths of 162 people with a further 432 being injured. This turned out to be the single most deadly German war time raid on Britain throughout the entire war.

Five years later on 22 June 1922, the war memorial was unveiled by Field Marshal Sir Henry Wilson who had played a prominent role during the war as a Staff Officer. In 1917 for example he was the military advisor to the Prime Minister David Lloyd George. In 1918 he became the Chief of the Imperial General Staff, remaining in that position after the war had finished, during a time which saw the British army greatly reduced in size, whilst still having to deal with growing unrest in the Middle East. He retired from the Army in 1922, having served his country for forty years. Having returned to his London home after the unveiling, he was shot dead by two members of the Irish

Republican Army. A memorial plaque in memory of Sir Henry, was unveiled a month after his death, next to the one he had unveiled at Liverpool Street Railway Station on the day he was killed.

The station also contains a memorial to another very brave individual. Captain Charles Algernon Fryatt of the Merchant Navy. On 28 March 1915, he was the captain of SS *Brussels*, a passenger ferry built in 1902 for the Great Eastern Railway, when he was ordered to stop by the German submarine *U-33*, commanded by Kapitanleutnant Konrad Gansser, near to the Maas light vessel. As *U-33* surfaced, Captain Fryatt decided to try and ram her, forcing her to crash dive to avoid a collision. In doing so Captain Fryatt made good his escape. For his actions that day Captain Fryatt was awarded a gold watch by the Admiralty with the following inscription.

'Presented by the Lords Commissioners of the Admiralty to Chas. Algernon Fryatt Master of the SS Brussels in recognition of the example set by that vessel when attacked by a German submarine on March 28th, 1915.'

Winston Churchill, who at the time was the First Lord of the Admiralty, had issued orders to all captains of British merchant vessels that they were to treat U-Boat crews as 'felons' and not prisoners of war and that if it were more convenient to do so, captains could shoot rather than take U-Boat crews prisoner. The order issued by Churchill also informed captains that if they surrendered their ships, they faced prosecution by the British government.

On 25 June 1916 SS *Brussels*, still with Captain Fryatt at her helm, set sail from the Hook of Holland on route to Harwich, England. Soon after leaving the Dutch port, she was surrounded by five German destroyers, the passengers were put to the life boats and the ship was escorted to Zeebrugge and then on to Bruges. Captain Fryatt and his crew had their personal belongings ceased and were then sent to a civilian internment camp at Ruhleben near Berlin. Having read the inscription on Fryatt's gold watch the German authorities decided that he should face a court martial, which was hastily arranged and took place on 27 July 1916, not, as one would imagine, in nearby Berlin, but in Bruges Town Hall in Belgium. Why, or who made this decision, is unclear. Captain Fryatt was found guilty of being a franc-tireur, which in essence means the Germans treated him as if he were a 'guerrilla fighter', and sentenced him to death by firing squad. The sentence was confirmed by the Kaiser and Fryatt was executed at 1900 hours the same day.

The Germans produced an execution notice in French, Dutch and German, but not English. It read as follows;

'The English Captain of a merchant ship, Charles Fryatt, of Southampton, though he did not belong to the armed forces of the enemy, attempted on March 28th, 1915, to destroy a German submarine by running it down. For this he has been condemned to death by judgement this day of the Field Court Martial of the Naval Corps, and has been executed. A ruthless deed has thus been avenged, belatedly but just.'

The notice was signed by the Admiral Commandant of the Naval Corps in Bruges, Von Schroder, and was dated 27 July 1916. Outside Germany, Captain Fryatt's execution caused disgust and disbelief, drawing politicians and newspapers to comment in England, America, Holland and Switzerland, to name but a few. The king wrote a personal letter to Captain Fryatt's widow expressing his indignation and abhorrence at her husband's execution. The Great Eastern Railway awarded Captain Fryatt's widow a pension of £250 a year which was increased by an extra £100 by the British government, an amazing amount of money at a time when a good average yearly working wage was not much more than £60–75.

In 1919 Captain Fryatt's body was exhumed and returned to England for reburial. His funeral took place at St Paul's Cathedral in the City of London on 8 July 1919, after which he was buried at All Saints' Church in Upper Dovercourt, Essex. The Belgian government posthumously awarded Captain Fryatt both the Belgian Order of Leopold and the Belgian Maritime War Cross. The sad irony about all of this is the implied suggestion that in a time of war it is acceptable for military personnel to kill or attempt to kill civilians, but not for those same individuals to be able to defend themselves against such an attack.

Another of the City's notable war memorials seen by thousands of people every day is the Mercantile Marine Memorial at Tower Hill, immediately opposite the Tower of London. It commemorates members of the Merchant Navy and fishing fleets who lost their lives during both the First and Second World Wars.

Merchant vessels were seen as fair game during the First World War, especially after Germany's policy of unrestricted submarine warfare came in to being in January 1917. By the end of the war a staggering 3,305 British merchant ships had been sunk with the loss of some 17,000 lives. The memorial was unveiled on 12 December 1928 by Queen Mary.

The National Submarine War Memorial, which was unveiled on 15 December 1922 by Admiral Sir Hugh Sinclair KCB, can be found on one of the walls of the Victoria Embankment opposite the Temple Underground station, and commemorates those sub-mariners who were killed in both world wars. The names of the fifty men who lost their lives during the First World War, and who have no known grave, are commemorated on two bronze panels on the left hand side of the memorial.

One of London's finest First World War memorials, can be found in the Great Hall at the Guildhall, Gresham Street, City of London. It was erected to commemorate the names of members and sons of members and officers of the City of London who fell in the Great War. It is located on the left hand side of the Dance Porch and has the names of one member, thirty-three sons of members, as well as seventy-eight staff of the City of London. It was unveiled on 20 January 1921 by the then Lord Mayor, James Roll, Esq.

Working on Smithfield Market provided the men employed there a really good education of life, because nearly everybody who worked on the market was a character in their own right. The place was buzzing all the time, a truly remarkable place to work. It was a place where men were hardy and fierce looking. They were strong and powerful from the hours and hours of lugging carts full of all kind of different meats up and down the market. Unloading a lorry load of beef quarters, pigs or a container full of frozen lambs, was like no other 'work out'. These men didn't need to go down the gym to exercise, they had done a workout before most people were even up and out of their beds in the morning.

The Smithfield Market War Memorial is dedicated to those people who were associated with the market who died during the First World

Smithfield Market War Memorial.

War. The names of the 212 individuals who are recorded on it, are inscribed on a granite block in gilded lead lettering which forms the main part of the ornately designed memorial. It was unveiled on 22 July 1921 by the Lord Mayor of London, J Roll Esq.

The memorial can be found in the middle of Smithfield Market in the City of London. The inscription on it says;

1914 – 1918
Remember with thanksgiving the true and faithful men
who in these years of war went forth from this place for.
God and the Right
The names of those who returned not again are here
inscribed to be honoured evermore.

The names of those recorded on it are as follows.

Adams, F E	Adams, Jack	Agass, Alfred
Alexander, S	Allen, L H	Allen, J
Anthony, George	Bagley, Alfred	Baker, Ben
Baker, Charles	Barber, W G	Barbero, E C
Batchelor, N V	Batts, W	Beer, H J
Berry, A	Berwick, William	Biscoe, J
Bowden, J	Bowyer, G H	Brackett, Arthur
Bradnum, B B	Briggs, Ernest	Bringloe, Ernest
Bristow, W G	Browne, Vernon R	Butler, H
Carter, Henry John	Cater, W	Cave, A
Champion, L S	Clarke, H	Collyer, W
Cooke, L F	Coombes, W E	Cossey, T
Coulthurst, Frank	Coulthurst, Temple	Covell, Howard
Crane, William George	Garrard, Joseph	Bates, T
Croft, William	Darvell, E	Day, H
Denniss, K G	Dickinson, W	Dixon, A
Dixon, W A	Dubock, H T	Dunmall, A J
Dyer, R L	Easton, Maurice	Edwards, A G
Edwards, Leonard	Elkins, C A	Elliot, Ernest
Elliot, Robert H	Ellison, W S	Fisk, Alfred
Fitzgibbon, F W	Flatley, George	Fountain, Leslie
Fowler, Arthur	Franks, H	Garnham, E A

Geeves, A	Gibson, T O	Gladwin, William
Glover, W E	Godfrey, Arthur	Gooding, A M
Gooding, H A	Gorick, S	Grace, W C
Grainger, R	Gray, W	Gray, R M
Graysmark, Frederick	Grice, L C	Griffin, H
Hall, Bert	Hall, Dick	Hannadine, H
Hunt, F	Hall, James	Hall, Walter
Hancock, Charles T	Hancock, W E	Hargrove, George
Hassall, L G	Hatton, A S	Hayes, F
Hayes, Arthur	Hayes, F	Hayhurst, J
Heslett, Sidney	Hilbert, G	Hilbert, H
Hodges, Harold	Holttum, A G	Hook, B
Horne, Arthur E	How, A E	Howell, F
Jannaway, H E	Jeffrey, A	Jenkins, Chas
Johnson, Guy F	Jones, G Taylor	Jones, William
Kablean, William C	Kennedy, W	Kentish, S L
Kew, W P	Jenkins, F E	Kime, G H E
Kingwell, Albert	Kirk, A J	Lee, L
Laws, A	Link, Horace A	Lloyd, F
Lock, S R T	Loughlin, M	Luxford, S
Lyons, R	Patten, Joseph	

Alfred Agass was a rifleman in the 2nd/11th Battalion, London Regiment (Finsbury Rifles), when he was killed in action on 18 September 1917 during fighting at the Third Battle of Ypres, which took place between 31 July and 10 November. He has no known grave and his name is commemorated on the Menin Gate Memorial at Ypres,.

Benjamin Barber Bradnum served as a corporal (3186) in the 11th Battalion, Middlesex Regiment when he died of his wounds on 23 October 1915 from wounds he received on 19 October. He was twenty-three years of age. He is buried in the Lillers Communal Cemetery in the Pas de Calais region of France.

Herbert Thomas Dubock was twenty-eight years of age and a private (026853) in the Royal Army Ordinance Corps, working out of the Base Depot, when he died of pneumonia. He is buried at Mikra British Cemetery, in the Kalamaria region of Greece.

The Ypres (Menin Gate) Memorial (Commonwealth War Graves Commission)

George Flatley was a private (GS/82441) in the 11th Battalion, City of London Regiment (Royal Fusiliers) originally having served as a private (70467) in the 106th Training Reserve Battalion. Although he served in a London Regiment he was in fact born and enlisted in Salford, Lancashire. It would appear that George was wounded during the Battle of Epehy which took place on 18 September 1918 and was part of the Allied hundred day offensive and the final push to victory. George died of his wounds on 19 September; he was only nineteen years of age and is buried at the Doingt Communal Cemetery Extension. Burials only took place at the cemetery between 5 September and the end of October 1918, but even in that comparatively short period of time, there were still 418 Commonwealth servicemen buried there.

Alfred M Gooding landed in France on 16 March 1915 as a private (18486) in the 1st Battalion, Grenadier Guards when he was killed in action on 10 September 1916 during the Battle of the Somme. He is buried in the Guards Cemetery at the village of Leboeufs, in the Somme region of France.

H A Gooding. was born in London but moved to Hampshire where he enlisted in to the Hampshire Regiment at Portsmouth as Private 1120, before later transferring to the 5th Battalion, Dorsetshire Regiment as Private 22114. He was killed in action on 16 September 1916 during the fighting at the Battle of the Somme.

There is a Frederick Thomas Graysmark recorded on the Commonwealth War Graves Commission website, who was killed in action on the Western Front on 3 May 1917, and is commemorated on the Arras Memorial which is situated in the Pas de Calais region of France. At the time of his death he was a twenty-four year old private (62588) in the 9th Battalion, London Regiment (Royal Fusiliers), but when he had initially enlisted at Westminster in London, he had joined the 3rd Battalion, City of London, Yeomanry as a Private (2705).

George Hargrove was a private (251636) in the 1st/3rd Battalion, London Regiment (Royal Fusiliers) when he was killed in action on 3 May 1917. He has no known grave and his name is commemorated on the Arras War Memorial, which forms part of the Faubourg D'Amiens Cemeter, in the Pas de Calais region of France.

William Hargrove served as a private (G/12473) in the 4th Battalion, Royal Fusiliers, when he was killed in action on 27 March 1916. He has no known grave and his name is commemorated on the Menin Gate Memorial at Ypres.

G and H Hilbert. The Commonwealth War Graves Commission shows only one person with that initial. A thirty year old man with the name of, Horace Ernest Hilbert who was a lance sergeant (5881) in the 3rd Battalion, Coldstream Guards, when he was killed less than a month into the war on 1 September. On that day, Horace and his comrades were fighting a rearguard action in the Foret de Retz to allow their colleagues from the 2nd Division to safely retreat.

Arthur George Holttum was a lance corporal (3006) in the 13th Battalion, London Regiment (Kensington) when he was killed in action on 21 February 1915. He is buried at the Estaires Communal Cemetery on the eastern outskirts of the town of Estaires.

H E Jannaway was a Corporal (203378) in the 1st Battalion, London Regiment (Royal Fusiliers). He was twenty-eight years of age when he was killed on 7 April 1917. He is buried at Achicourt Road Cemetery in the Pas de Calais region of France. It was a little used cemetery by either Commonwealth or Allied Units, and in the main only for a four month period between March and June 1917 and mainly consists of officers and men from the London Regiment.

William Charles Kablean was a private (252488) in the 3rd Battalion, London Regiment (Royal Fusiliers) when he was killed in action on 24 August 1917; he was twenty-four years of age. He is buried at the Duhallow Advanced Dressing Station Cemetery in the West-Vlaanderen region of Belgium.

Gilbert Henry Ernest Kime was a second lieutenant in No. 10 Squadron, Royal Air Force, when he died aged twenty-four. He was the holder of a Military Medal. He is buried in the Woodgrange Park Cemetery in East Ham

Hurbert Sidney Macbeth was a private (511005) in the 1st/4th Battalion, London Regiment (London Scottish) when he was killed in action on the very first day of the Battle of the Somme when Commonwealth forces suffered an estimated 50,000 casualties, 20,000 of whom were killed. He has no known grave and his name is commemorated on the Thiepval Memorial.

Reginald Zani was a gunner (166330) in the 157th Siege Battery, Royal Garrison Artillery, when he was killed in action on 11 December 1917. He was twenty-two years of age. He is buried in the Lijssenthoek Military Cemetery in the West-Vlaanderen region of Belgium. The cemetery is the second largest Commonwealth cemetery in Belgium.

Arthur Edward Urlwin and William James Snow Urlwin were brothers, with William being the elder by some five years. Both Arthur and William worked as clerks at Smithfield Meat Market, whist their father Walter, also worked there, but as a scalesman. Arthur was a lance corporal (22996) in 'Y' Company, 17th (1st South East Lancashire) Battalion, Lancashire Fusiliers when he was killed in action on 3 March 1918. He was twenty-eight years of age. His name is commemorated on the Tyne Cot Memorial, in the West-Vlaanderen region of Belgium. William James Snow Urlwin was thirty-four years of age when he died of his wounds on 29 October 1918. He was a lance bombardier (108916) in the 129th Heavy Battery, Royal Garrison Artillery who had first landed in France on 27 March 1916. He is buried at the Awoingt British Cemetery which is in a small village in the Nord region of France, just a few kilometres away from the town of Cambrai. The cemetery wasn't begun until the latter half of October 1918, hence making William one of the very first to be buried there.

Henry Charles Marrison was a thirty-five year old private (3/3514) in the 1st Battalion, Essex Regiment when he was killed in action during fighting at Gallipoli on 7 May 1915. The Allies, which included Henry's Battalion, had only landed on the peninsula eleven days earlier on 25/26 April 1915 and had almost immediately been thrown into action against determined Turkish defenders who had the advantage over their attackers by holding the high ground. Henry's name is commemorated on the Helles Memorial in Turkey along with the names of 21,000 other Commonwealth servicemen who lost their lives during fighting on the peninsula.

A W Polyblank was a private (94837) in the Royal Army Medical Corp when he died on 5 March 1919. He is buried at the City of London and Tower Hamlets Cemetery in London.

Bernard Oppenheim served as a rifleman (R/30139) in the 10th Battalion, Kings Royal Rifle Corps when he was killed on 30 November 1917 during the Battle of Cambrai. His name is commemorated on the Cambrai Memorial which is situated at Louveval, which is a small village in the Nord region of France.

Henry Oppenheim was a lance corporal (40973) in 7th/8th Battalion,

Roya Inniskilling Fusiliers, when he was killed in action on 23 March 1918. His name is commemorated on the Pozieres Memorial in the village of Pozieres on the outskirts of the neighbouring town of Albert. It was unveiled on 4 August 1930 by Sir Horace Smith-Dorrien, who sadly died just eight days after the unveiling.

Dudley William Arthur Mitchener was serving as a twenty-one year old private (350501) in 'C' Company, 7th Battalion, London Regiment, when he died of his wounds on 9 June 1917 during the Battle of Messines. He is buried in the Lijssenthoek Military Cemetery near Poperinge in the West-Vlaanderen region of Belgium.

Tower Hamlets cemetery contains the graves of 205 Commonwealth servicemen who died during the First World War. Of these, 69 had died after the signing of Armistice on 11 November 1918, indicating that they died either as a result of their injuries or from illness or disease. There is also a City of London Cemetery and Crematorium, but it is located some miles away from the City, in Manor Park. Most of the servicemen who are buried there died whilst being treated at the Bethnal Green Military Hospital.

Tower Hamlets Cemetery & War Memorial (Commonwealth War Games Commission)

The Royal Fusiliers Monument can be found at High Holborn in the City of London where its boundaries meet with the adjoining Borough of Camden. It was unveiled by the Lord Mayor of the City of London on Saturday 4 November 1922 and is a dedication to the 22,000 men of the Royal Fusiliers who died whilst serving with the Regiment during the First World War. Although the figure on the Memorial is said to commemorate a Sergeant Cox, who served with the Royal Fusiliers throughout the war, it actually depicts a private wearing his service uniform.

The statue which sits on top of a pedestal of Portland stone, which is over sixteen feet in height, is made of bronze and is over eight feet tall. All of the Battalions, whether Regular, Service or Territorial, which served in the First World War, are commemorated on one side of the pedestal. Originally the memorial was intended to sit in one of the capital's eight Royal Parks. That idea was changed to Hounslow Barracks before eventually ending up in its present location at Holborn.

Royal Fusiliers War Memorial.

The Court of Common Council met up in 1919 to help commemorate the men from the City of London who were killed during the First World War. They decided on a monument. The approval of the eventual design and its cost came from the Joint Committee of the City and County of London. Sir Aston Webb was the architect who was chosen to design the memorial, the building of which was then a joint effort between Alfred Drury, who was responsible for the bronze statues and Mr W S Frith, who took care of the stone work and carving.

The London Troops War Memorial sits in front of the Royal Exchange in the City of London. It commemorates the London Regiments and Battalions, including those from the City of London, who fought in the First World War. The memorial is made out of Portland stone and there are two life-size bronze statues of a soldier one on either side of the main column. One represents the Royal Fusiliers and the other the Royal Field Artillery. The cost of the memorial was £7,000, the monies for which were raised by public subscription, at the nearby Mansion House in 1919, coming mainly from the City's banks and guilds, during which time the Mayor of the City of London was Sir Horace Brooks Marshall.

Prince Albert, the Duke of York, unveiled the statue and the prestige of being the guard of honour went to the 3rd Battalion, Grenadier Guards, who also provided their regimental band for the occasion. The day of the unveiling was 12 November 1920, and although a memorable occasion for all in attendance, the weather was also notable for being foggy.

The inscription on the memorial that relates to the First World War, reads as follows.

'To the immortal honour of the officers, non-commissioned officers and men of London who served their King and Empire in the Great War 1914-1919.
This memorial is dedicated in proud & grateful recognition by the City and the County of London.
Their name liveth for evermore.
Unveiled on Nov 12th 1920
by HRH the Duke of York on behalf of
Field-Marshal HRH the Duke of Connaught KG, KT, KP.'

Postscript:
The Aftermath of War

After the signing of the Armistice in November 1918, the City of London quickly returned to being the City of London; it was, after all, the financial heartbeat of Great Britain, and undoubtedly one of the biggest such centres in the world. Thankfully, because of Kaiser Wilhelm's order that the City of London would not to be targeted, it had suffered only very minor damage from Zeppelin and Gotha air raids, so there was no major rebuilding programme needed before the metropolis could return to normality.

For those who lived in the City of London, there were the same social and economic issues to deal with as everywhere else in the country, affecting most aspects of life. People had more expectation for an improvement in their personal well-being as well as a better world to live in for future generations. Nobody wanted to look back to before the war and think about how life was for them. Especially with the memories of four years of bloody and brutal war still fresh in the forefront of their minds. Everybody had been affected by the war in some way shape or form and with victory people now expected and wanted more out of life.

With the war won, history would record the dawning of a new age. Empires had not only fallen they had been obliterated and those that hadn't had also seen changes. Land had been lost and gained, freedoms had been sought by impoverished nations and revolutions had changed some nations forever. If the ideals for which Great Britain and her Allies fought for were sincere and not merely the whim of a passing hour, then it was upon these that the character of the new world, had to be built upon for a better tomorrow.

For some the simplicity of the thought of food and when the end of rationing would come about, were at the forefront of their thinking. The war years had seen the Defence of the Realm Act (DORA) control most aspects of life, including what people could and couldn't eat; people had become so used to the restraints, some couldn't remember a time without them.

People were starting to think about such niceties as getting away from the City and going for a visit or on holiday to one of the many coastal towns throughout Kent and Essex. For others it was the return of sports and the crowds at football matches, cricket with its lazy long days slowly meandering through the day, horse racing at Ascot, Goodwood or Epsom whilst quaffing glass after glass of champagne or the niceties which went with the Henley Regatta or a weekend at Cowes. An article in the *Essex Newsman* dated Saturday 8 February 1919, showed how the memories of the war were never that far away for most people, and that in some cases there simply never was any justice for those who most deserved it.

£125 for a Son

'In the City of London Court on Monday £125 was awarded to Arthur Weller, green grocer, South Benfleet, and his wife, for the death of their son Archibald, late chief bedroom steward on board the SS *Llandovery Castle*, which was torpedoed by a U-Boat on June 27. His earnings were £11 10s per month.'

What the article didn't explain was that at the time she was sunk, the vessel was actually being used as a Canadian hospital ship. She was en route from Halifax in Nova Scotia, Canada to Liverpool, when she was sunk off of the south coast of Ireland. In total, 234 patients, doctors and nurses lost their lives when the ship was sunk. The incident was made worse when the German submarine that had sunk the *Llandovery Castle*, the *SM U-86,* surfaced, sank all of the lifeboats and machine gunned the survivors in an effort to leave no witnesses to the atrocity. Twenty-four people did survive and were later able to give evidence against the submarine's captain, Helmut Brummer-Patzig.

In 1921 Brummer-Patzig manage to evade conviction for the atrocity. Before his trial in Leipzig, he fled the country taking himself out of German jurisdiction. When the Second World War began, he returned to Germany, becoming a Commander of a U-Boat training unit. He never faced any sanction for his wartime atrocity. For those who lost loved ones with the sinking of the *Llandovery Castle*, they suffered for a second time with the knowledge that the man responsible for their deaths, would not be punished for his crimes.

The War to End Wars was over; happily for those celebrating the return to normality or what would pass for it could not see into the future. For those of us now, with the benefit of hindsight, their celebrations are hollow. Many of the children waving their banners and the young men and women cheering the troops home would, in another twenty years, be victims of another conflict, bloodier than they could imagine.

Sources

www.fany.org.uk
www.cwgc.org
www.20thcenturylondon.org
www.ancestry.co.uk
www.1914-1918.net www.cityoflondon.gov.uk
www.bbc.co.uk
www.meaningsofservice1914.qmul.ac.uk
www.ezitis.myzen.co.uk
www.stephen-stratford.co.uk
www.britishnewspaperarchive.co.uk
www.kingscollections.org
www.battlefields1418.50megs.com
www.postalheritage.org.uk
www.parliament.uk
www.wrecksite.eu
De Ruvigny's Roll of Honour 1914-1919
www.bankofengland.co.uk/archive
www.bedfordregiment.org.uk
www.historylearningsite.co.uk
www.westernfrontassociation.com
www.spartacus-education.com
www.powell76.talktalk.net
MANNING-FOSTER, AE *The National Guard in the Great War
1914-1918* Cope and Fenwick, London, 1920
SIMKINS, Peter, *Kitchener's Army – The Raising of the New Army
1914-1916*. Pen and Sword, Barnsley, 2007
WILSON, Constance A *Those Were The Days* Unknown publisher,
1949

Index